Affected Labour in a Café Culture

What does it mean to work in the 'hip' postmodern economy? This book develops the concept of 'affected labour' within Melbourne, Australia. Through the lens of café and bar culture, the book provides an ethnographic investigation into the ways that affect arises, circulates, sticks and dissipates over the course of everyday encounters.

The dynamics and atmospheres of affective labour among those working in the hospitality-oriented environments are unfolded. Service work is rooted in the notion that labour is 'performed' by an exhausted worker for a demanding customer. This book goes beyond this idea by describing the way not only consumers are moved by the experience and seduced by the atmosphere, but more pressingly workers and employers.

This book reveals the ways in which workers themselves are capitalised on by *being* affected pleasurably in the moment, fuelling an economy of short-term desires in which 'affected labourers' are manipulated.

Alexia Cameron continues to develop and refine her practice in sociology. Her work is interested in the intersections between affect and emotion; work, production and economy; and postmodern cultures. She can be contacted at: a.m.cameron@hotmail.com.

Routledge Research in Culture, Space and Identity
Series editor: Dr. Jon Anderson, School of Planning and
Geography, Cardiff University, UK

The *Routledge Research in Culture, Space and Identity Series* offers a forum for original and innovative research within cultural geography and connected fields. Titles within the series are empirically and theoretically informed and explore a range of dynamic and captivating topics. This series provides a forum for cutting-edge research and new theoretical perspectives that reflect the wealth of research currently being undertaken. This series is aimed at upper-level undergraduates, research students and academics, appealing to geographers as well as the broader social sciences, arts and humanities.

For a full list of titles in this series, please visit www.routledge.com/Routledge-Research-in-Culture-Space-and-Identity/book-series/CSI

Arts in Place: The Arts, the Urban and Social Practice
Cara Courage

Explorations in Place Attachment
Jeffrey S. Smith

Geographies of Digital Culture
Edited by Tilo Felgenhauer and Karsten Gäbler

The Nocturnal City
Robert Shaw

Geographies of Making, Craft and Creativity
Edited by Laura Price and Harriet Hawkins

Spaces of Spirituality
Edited by Nadia Bartolini, Sara MacKian and Steve Pile

Affected Labour in a Café Culture: The Atmospheres and Economics of 'Hip' Melbourne
Alexia Cameron

Affected Labour in a Café Culture

The Atmospheres and Economics of 'Hip' Melbourne

Alexia Cameron

Routledge
Taylor & Francis Group

LONDON AND NEW YORK

First published 2018 by Routledge

2 Park Square, Milton Park, Abingdon, Oxfordshire OX14 4RN
52 Vanderbilt Avenue, New York, NY 10017

Routledge is an imprint of the Taylor & Francis Group, an informa business

First issued in paperback 2020

Copyright © 2018 Alexia Cameron

The right of Alexia Cameron to be identified as author of this work has been
asserted by her in accordance with sections 77 and 78 of the Copyright,
Designs and Patents Act 1988.

All rights reserved. No part of this book may be reprinted or reproduced or
utilised in any form or by any electronic, mechanical, or other means, now
known or hereafter invented, including photocopying and recording, or in any
information storage or retrieval system, without permission in writing from
the publishers.

Notice:
Product or corporate names may be trademarks or registered trademarks, and
are used only for identification and explanation without intent to infringe.

British Library Cataloguing-in-Publication Data
A catalogue record for this book is available from the British Library

Library of Congress Cataloging-in-Publication Data
A catalog record has been requested for this book

ISBN: 978-0-8153-8004-7 (hbk)
ISBN: 978-0-367-59210-3 (pbk)

Typeset in Times New Roman
by Swales & Willis Ltd, Exeter, Devon, UK

Contents

Acknowledgements

I am so appreciative of the venues and individual workers who generously partook in this study and welcomed me into their working worlds. I extend my gratitude to La Trobe University for offering me the opportunity of PhD candidature and a postgraduate research scholarship, without which this research would not have been possible. I feel fortunate to have worked under the principal supervision of Dr Anne-Maree Sawyer and co-supervision of Dr Sara James and Dr Ray Madden. I am especially grateful to Prof Gregory Seigworth and Dr Benjamin Snyder for their generous and thoughtful feedback. I am thankful to my love, Daniel, who has shown me unconditional support throughout this project—our running dialogue and shared observations, over the years, meant the research stayed 'alive' in me.

1 Being moved in immaterial economies

Work and self in the precarious postmodern

I'm sitting in a chaotic café during the lunch rush; it feels like a high-school lunch hall type of atmosphere. There is, ironically, no music playing despite the fact that we're in a highly affective café space with a minimalist design; whitewashed walls, wall-to-wall shelving on which stand indoor plants, plenty of wood veneer, simple refined menus with Helvetica-font type, marble and rose gold, etc. I'm one of six customers jammed into a shared table, to the right of a large marbled counter/coffee-making area, and, honestly, it is extremely difficult to relax. As I hunch on my stool observing the café space for my first session of fieldwork, I watch three workers separately approach a table of diners and offer them menus, even though they had already ordered their food and coffees the first time. The customers didn't seem too concerned, though, as they resumed taking romantic 'selfies' together. Another worker begins casually strolling around the packed café 'floor' talking on her iPhone, mid-service, while another table of four customers are being assured by the worker—during the characteristic preponderance associated with choosing a type of coffee these days—"All our coffee is special!" In a drawn-out, satirical tone, she quips, "*But*, if you ask nicely, we may have something under the bar for you to taste . . ." In this café, it was if they were busy enough to make you, as the customer, feel lucky to be there. That the service was remarkably average in a world-renowned industry, predicated on wowing customers with ever more refined and atmospheric variations on a very similar product, is illustrative of the 'hip' gentrification of precarious work in postmodernity. This book explores what it means to be affected for a living in 'hip' Melbourne cafés and bars. While most workers appeared to easily detach from the multitude of unpleasant encounters that they had with "shit customers", as is illustrated above, it was the far less frequent moments of ephemeral and authentic joy that seduced them significantly more intensely (Sam, a barista and one of my interviewees—all of the workers' names in this book are pseudonyms). Through building the concept of 'affected labour', this book describes how patterns of feeling and ecologies of interaction—within the production of seduction—create immaterial value, reproduce 'hipness', and inform desires.

The postmodern person, says Christopher Lasch (1979, p. 93), has grown so self-aware of their public persona and exteriorised identity that they long "for the lost innocence of spontaneous feeling". Individuals living in the postmodern "seek the kind of approval that applauds not their actions but their personal attributes. They wish to be not so much esteemed as admired" (Lasch 1979, p. 59). Lasch (1979) relates the hollowness of inauthentic, or narcissistic postmodern experiences, to declining tradition, globalisation, advancements in mass communication technology, the end of history, and, as he emphasises most, the erosion of traditional measures of skill across the labour market. He explains that the traditional understanding of skill required in industrial work, like the transparency of job allocation on the assembly line, has blurred and led to post-industrial "conditions in which labor power takes the form of personality rather than strength or intelligence", in what he describes as "a kind of absurdist theatre of the self" (Lasch 1979, p. 92, p. 90). Richard Sennett (1998), too, in his critical work *The Corrosion of Character: The Personal Consequences of Work in the New Capitalism*, describes postmodern people as embodying a collage of identities and thus remaining ever open to new experiences. He says, "the psyche dwells in a state of endless becoming—a selfhood which is never finished" (Sennett 1998, p. 133). Explaining postmodernity in terms of the incoherence in people's life narratives, the author describes the postmodern person as "a pliant self, a collage of fragments unceasing in its becoming, ever open to new experience—these are just the psychological conditions suited to short term work experience, flexible institutions, and constant risk-taking" (Sennett 1998, p. 133). Jean-François Lyotard (1984), as well, hypothesises Sennett's (1998) depiction of scattered postmodern identities in terms of the end of grand stories and ideologies that are replaced, in postmodernity, with multiplying petit or little narratives.

Indeed, numerous scholars describe similar accounts of the end of Enlightenment certainties (May 2011). Ulrich Beck (1992) sees the end of Enlightenment certainty reflected in the rise of multiple individual biographies, ever more vulnerable to the seductive myth of individualism, or what he calls a *risk society*. Anthony Giddens (1991), too, describes the intensely uncertain postmodern condition as *ontological insecurity*, where people increasingly live in an almost existential state of perpetual anxiety as to where they stand and where they are going tomorrow. Thus, the challenge for the ontologically insecure, Giddens (1991) suggests, is their capacity to keep a stable narrative going—what he terms the *narrative biography*. And, in their critical work *The New Spirit of Capitalism*, Luc Boltanski and Eve Chiapello (2007) tell us that contemporary capitalism entails inventive, creative, and imaginative workers who can communicate effectively, especially within a group, as well as synthesise and filter the information overload brought about by technological acceleration. Traditional skills and qualifications that once dictated labour-market entry increasingly come secondary to experience, indebtedness or passion, social skills, and networking.

Postmodern conditions are intimately linked with neoliberalism and the democratisation of self-expression—where the individual is expected to redefine the structural constraints that they are faced with. In her insightful work

Coming Up Short: Working-Class Adulthood in an Age of Uncertainty, Jennifer Silva (2013) explores the *mood economy* in postmodern working-class American culture. The neoliberal logic in postmodern working-class narratives, the author describes, were rooted in a belief that the uncertainty of the present could be rationalised through a coming-of-age narrative that was based on self-transformation and self-management. Many participants in Silva's (2013) study, for example, felt betrayed by their parents who had promised them a stable future by going to university and yet they found themselves still unemployed, or in precarious and low-paid labour, even after completing tertiary study. Others felt let down, because their parents hadn't prioritised their needs when they were younger, especially their psychological needs, leading them to self-diagnose on the internet through intense self-monitoring—seeing themselves as solely responsible for liberating themselves from their conditions. The participants in Silva's (2013, p. 149) study internalised the external constraints of their past—seeing their feelings as a matter of individual responsibility, and being untrusting of social institutions and "hardened to the world around them". Dignity in the *mood economy* is to be found in "emotional self-management rather than in traditional accomplishments such as marriage or work"; the past, from the perspectives of the participants in Silva's (2013, p. 150) study, involved stories of a history of struggle that only they could "fix". Trapped inside themselves and unable to see their futures, they used their past as way of negotiating with, and making sense of, the treacherous present; hence, the author concludes: "[f]or these young men and women, risk is radically privatized" (Silva 2013, p. 146).

Paolo Virno (2007) suggests that neoliberal individualism produces growing expressions of cynicism in contemporary life. This cynicism, he says, is the result of absent principles of equivalence in immaterial production and the new lateral division of labour. The author extrapolates that while, during the early stages of industrial capitalism, there was ensured transparency in the production process and in the Fordist division of labour, given the more limited knowledge businesses had of extracting surplus value from the capitalist transaction, there was at least a predictable principle of equivalence. The goods being produced in industrial production—like cars and typewriters—were transparent in their material value, and made by manual labourers whose work was measured and awarded according to an obsessively calculated and streamlined division of labour, like *scientific management* (Lazzarato 2006, p. 137). In postmodern production, however, use-value is the main source of surplus being produced, where value is drawn out of desires that manifest outside the capitalist transaction, in everyday life, and "the life of the mind" (Virno 2004, p. 49). The erosion of transparent measures of value, for Virno (2007), constitutes the basis of a contemporary cynicism in conditions where transparency is denied. Hence the author says: "the principle of equivalence used to be the foundation of the most rigid hierarchies and ferocious inequalities, yet it ensured a sort of visibility in the social nexus" (Virno 2007, pp. 6–7). Virno (2007) argues, as use-value becomes increasingly abstract, and measures of determining value ever more camouflaged, postmodern people become cynical toward the possibility of transparent indicators in their lives more generally.

Accordingly, they abandon their demand for equality, perhaps turning narcissistically inward as Lasch (1979) posited, vulnerable to the myth of individualism—that they are accountable and the market is not (Virno 2007).

Work in postmodernity can be broadly considered in terms of two significant changes to *conditions* of labour: transformations to the working day and growing precariousness. It is not that work extends over different spaces per se, in multiplied islands of production; rather it is that "the temporality of life becomes governed by work"—that which Michael Hardt and Antonio Negri (2004) describe as "living labour" (Gill & Pratt 2008, p. 17). As the authors illuminate:

> when production is aimed at solving a problem, [. . .] or creating an idea or a relationship, work time tends to expand to entire time of life. An idea or image comes to you not only in the office, but also in the shower or in your dreams.
> (Hardt & Negri 2004, pp. 111–112)

Like many social scientists have pointed to, since the 1970s, in such terms as *post-industrialism, post-Fordism, the knowledge economy*, and so on, the older industrial division of labour has grown horizontally so that there is less of a gap between lower and upper tears of traditional organisational hierarchies (Gill & Pratt 2008, p. 2). Coupled with this decentralisation and flattening of traditional hierarchies as defining contemporary production, the service and information sectors have steadily increased, leaving Fordist and later Taylorist measures of productivity increasingly abstract, because the line between work and non-work continues to erode (Hardt & Negri 2000; Lazzarato 2006). For example, let's say production is aimed at solving a problem or encouraging a customer to purchase an iPhone 8, rather than the previous model. This lived element rapidly seeps outside the working environment and formal working hours, into the labourer's own archive of experience and their capacity to affect and to be affected. This is because, to do the job effectively, the labourer must draw from the archive of their own experience living in the world in their journey to affect the customer, rendering their private life and fabric of mind a lucrative source of value (Hardt 1999). As Virno (2007, p. 5) describes clearly, "what is learned, carried out, and consumed in the time outside of labour is then utilised in the production of commodities".

Attached to "the temporality of life being governed by work" is the rise in precarious working arrangements (Gill & Pratt 2008, p. 17). Precariousness refers to a widely-felt experience encompassed by all forms of insecure, flexible, contingent, illegal, casual, and temporary employment, as well as freelancing or working from home (Gill & Pratt 2008). In other words, precariousness refers just as much to the CEO as it does to the low-paid janitor or the self-employed researcher, so it's broad enough to capture the commonality of disenfranchised experiences irrespective of traditional homogenising categories that people might fit into. In their perceptive article 'Precarity: A Savage Journey to the Heart of Embodied Capitalism', Vassilis Tsianos and Dimitris Papadopoulos (2006, p. 5) explain precariousness in terms of the "in the meantime" of contemporary life, where the common expression "I don't have time" symbolises "the almost existential condition of vulnerability felt as a constant state of being in every moment of everyday life". In other words, precariousness exploits, because it operates according to flexibility and 'the moment', so that the future is not guaranteed and, as such, the future is exploited (Tsianos & Papadopoulos 2006). Brian Massumi (2015, pp. 200–201), similarly, tells us that the lack of equilibrium felt by post-modern people means that "crisis and catastrophe are no longer exceptional, they're the normal situation [. . .] we're absorbed in the immanence of catastrophe, always braced for it". Adaptability, resilience, and flexibility have become the key elements required in precarious contemporary life, framed positively in such popular neoliberal idioms as 'living in the moment', 'seizing the moment', and 'time is money' (Silva 2013; Tsianos & Papadopoulos 2006).

Tsianos and Papadopoulos (2006) suggest a rethinking of the properly capital-ist relationship between productivity and private property, because postmodern work—especially *immaterial labour*—increasingly takes advantage of workers' private lives, that is, their private property. The endless resources of the work-er's mind are relied upon for productivity and, yet, this unrestricted access that employers have is not acknowledged in the labour market, thus ignoring the core capitalist principle of private property. For example, while goods are privatised in capitalism (in order to extract profit from them), the worker's mind and their pro-pensity to feel *are not recognised as private property*. If the worker's subjectivity is *not* a tool for capitalists from which to derive value and productivity, "it breaks the immediate flow of time, it becomes frightening because it escapes the dom-inance of the immaterial linear chronocracy" (Tsianos & Papadopoulos, 2006, p. 5). Potential for postmodern workers, the authors suggest, lies in their ability to harness the logic of precariousness—by manipulating the present moment or "tar-rying with time"—and, in doing so, denying the employer endless access to the life of their mind (Tsianos & Papadopoulos 2006, p. 5; Virno 2004). Similarly, for Virno (2007), postmodernity requires an emphasis on intellectualising the faculty to think and imagine through practising autonomy, and ordering one's feelings in the 'heat of the moment', rather than intelligence being understood as an outcome produced by thought, in the form of, say, a degree qualification, or the outcome of consuming something; *intelligence is in the act of thinking in the moment*. Hardt and Negri, too, explain:

> Language, for example, like affects and gestures, is for the most part com-mon, and indeed if language were made either private or public—that is, if large portions of our words, phrases, or parts of speech were subject to pri-vate ownership or public authority—then language would lose its powers of expression, creativity, and communication.
>
> (2009, p. ix)

The same skills workers are required to possess—flexibility, ordering of affects, resisting seduction, personal investment/commitment—transgress the confines of work and are, in many ways, essential skills for life in postmodernity (Eden 2012).

In her critical work *The Managed Heart: Commercialization of Human Feeling*, Arlie Hochschild (1983) examines emotion and selfhood in the context of service work, describing *emotional labour* as the employee's regulation of feeling within paid employment for the ultimate gain of that employer. Hochschild ethnographically situates her concept of *emotional labour* by observing the labour performed by air hosts and hostesses in the burgeoning American airline industry of the 1980s. Influenced by both Karl Marx (1993) and Erving Goffman (1959), she argues that the emotional life of workers was increasingly governed by the organisations they worked for, eventually rendering their emotions less and less spontaneous and authentic in both private *and* public life. The governing of emotion, in Hochschild's (1983) research of the *emotional labour* undertaken by air hosts and hostesses, illuminates the disconnection, or estrangement, between a person's sense of self and the relevance of their feelings. Inspired by Goffman's (1959) explanation of the conflict between the mask-wearing performance, and the experience of inner turmoil within social interaction, and Marx's (1993) description of the worker's alienation from their species-being or creative essence, Hochschild (1983) argues that the *emotion work* implicit in private life parallels the *emotional labour* required in public life. The double edge, she explains, is that when workers engaged in *surface acting* at work, which is other-directed and *performed emotional labour*, workers felt negative feelings of inauthenticity. And, when they engaged in *deep acting* in their private lives—as inner-directed and self-regulatory *emotion work*—they found themselves burnt out by the combination of inauthenticity or insincerity, as well as the emotional stress of directing work and feelings inwardly. *Emotional labourers*, Hochschild (1983) concludes, are often alienated from their own feelings brought about by the commercialisation of emotion in the new economy.

This awkward tension between work and selfhood in postmodernity is captured well in Anthony Lloyd's (2012) analysis of the tension faced by call centre workers, who embodied the ideologies of consumer society and sought authenticity and meaning in their work, and, at the same time, felt no personal attachment or identification with their jobs at the call centre. Lloyd (2012, p. 630) exposes a key tension, inasmuch as, "the economic and political necessities of cultural capitalism and liberal democracy require us to believe that our current system of governance can offer us everything we want from life", with the reality for workers in his study of a "cynical, pessimistic awareness of the social position they find themselves in" (Lloyd 2012, p. 632). While work remained central to everyday life for the workers in Lloyd's (2012, p. 632) study, there was nothing they identified with in call centre work per se, because they often felt stuck in a cycle of consumption, disillusionment, desiring, and "living in the present". Indeed, most workers embodied the values of consumer society—a toxic attachment to temporary relief in shops and in bars—which became engrained in their *habitus* (Lloyd 2012).

While most participants in Lloyd's (2012) study found very little meaning in the long-term trajectory of the job, they did find meaning in the job's temporary usefulness in allowing them to survive while "contemplating" their future plans or "real careers" (Lloyd 2012, p. 628). But "living in the present", for many workers, meant a toxic attachment to consumerism and the allure of short-term gratification:

> Those respondents who were vague when contemplating the future preferred to live for the present and assert their status on a field they could compete on; the night-time economy and through the consumer spending their meagre wages offered. Work was something to be endured in order to go out at the weekend or indulge in shopping sprees.
>
> (Lloyd 2012, p. 631)

The uncertainty and insecurity, and in Lloyd's words "unsatisfying experiences of work" (2012, p. 631), lead them to pursue more identifiable environments that provide them with pleasure. These pornographic cycles of pleasure-seeking behaviour carried by contemporary consumer society, he concludes, mean, "for many of my respondents, their lives are characterised by frequent circles of optimistic visions of a bright future and a cynical, pessimistic awareness of the social position they find themselves in" (Lloyd 2012, p. 632). Rational self-interest in late capitalist ideology—as a matter of common sense—means that the structural limitations and failures are considered secondary to the power of the individual in overpowering circumstance (Schutz 1953; Silva 2013).

In pursuit of 'life-value': the ascendency of immaterial production

The internalisation of feelings induced in the postmodern market environment—blurring the lines between work and self—is intensified by the commodification of immaterial goods and services, or *immaterial labour*.

> Since the production of services results in no material and durable good, we define the labour involved in this production as *immaterial* labour—that is, labour that produces an immaterial good, such as a service, a cultural product, knowledge, or communication.
>
> (Hardt & Negri 2000 p. 290, emphasis in original)

On the one hand, *immaterial labour* is immediately intellectual or linguistic in its production of information, for example: problem solving, linguistic expressions, communication, and analytical tasks are all what Maurizio Lazzarato (2006) describes as the "informational content" of the immaterial commodity, and which Hardt and Negri (2000) theorise as *informational labour* (Gill & Pratt 2008, p. 7). *Informational labourers* are increasingly faced with the challenges of a rampant techno-capitalism; they are expected to be masters of self-governed upskilling and, attached to this, they must be excellent communicators (Hardt & Negri 2000). In her important book *Work's Intimacy*, Melissa Gregg (2011) explores the impact of techno-capitalism on both work *and* private life through the growing use of the technology in the contemporary office, which consequently renders work an ever more intimate experience. The paradox Gregg (2011) identifies is that for all the cost-saving, time-saving, and waste-saving benefits of new technology on the contemporary *informational labourer*, such benefits create a whole new subset of problems because technology dominates simultaneously in people's private *and* working lives. The importance of emailing well is a requirement of *informational labourers'* skillset that is not confined to the workplace. Yet, effective email writing, and organising time to receive and then reply to emails, tends to be the sole responsibility of the individual worker and hinged upon their own linguistic and cultural resources, which are unaccounted and unacknowledged by employers.

On the other hand, but not in opposition because they often converge, *immaterial labour* produces what Lazzarato (2006) describes as the "cultural content" of the immaterial commodity, and which Hardt and Negri (2000) theorise as *affective labour* (Gill & Pratt 2008, p. 8). The authors introduce *affective labour* by comparing it with care work or feminist analyses of "women's work" (Hardt & Negri 2000, p. 274). While in an obvious sense care work and service work, more broadly, are immersed in the atmospheres of somatic, corporeal, and emotional intensity, this obviousness renders care work the clearest way into the concept (Hardt & Negri 2000). *Affective labour* is that which manipulates and produces an affect as "labour in the bodily mode" (Hardt & Negri 2000, p. 293). Michel Foucault's (2003) conception of *biopolitics*, where power and governance express themselves through the body, as outlined in his collection of essays titled *Society Must Be Defended* (1975–1976), informed Hardt and Negri's (2000, p. 293) concept of *affective labour* as "labour in the bodily mode". Foucault (2003) understands regimes of power and governance as visceral and immaterial forces that manifest themselves in the body. This inspired the field of post-structural philosophy to refocus its lens on ontology, nature, and the body, largely attributable to Foucault's (1990, 2003) positioning of the body and senses as primary agents of power and governance. Both *affective* and *informational labour* involve activities concerned with "defining and fixing cultural and artistic standards, fashions, tastes, consumer norms, and, more strategically, public opinion" (Lazzarato 2006, p. 133). In Hardt and Negri's (2000, p. xiii) words, *affective* and *informational labour* are what drive "the postmodernization of the global economy".

Just as the dominance of factory production during early industrialism seeped into everyday life and the cultural logic more generally, as factory workers became consumers of the products that their labour produced, today *immaterial labour* is in the same hegemonic position as industrial labour was a century ago. Like the factory infiltrated the social logic, people developed industrial time consciousness: they ran their households like divisions of labour, and their emotions were largely rationalised in accordance with the dominant production model of Fordism, and later Taylorism (Hardt & Negri 2000). Today, the labour required in immaterial production mirrors the elements involved in conscious life so that life itself has been "put to work" (Eden 2012; Gill & Pratt 2008, p. 15; Hardt & Negri 2000). The very tasks required of such workers—being affected by the customer/brand/workplace, writing an email well, making a brand emotionally contagious, thinking in the moment, teaching affectively, communicating a 'hip' vibe, or generating and regenerating the workplace's ethos and symbols—are lucrative skills that directly produce relationships and social life; *capital becomes geared toward the production of social relations* (Hardt & Negri 2000). *Affective* and *informational labour* present the two dominant modes of *immaterial labour* influencing other modes of production, because what is fashioned embodies and reproduces "form[s]-of-life" (Hardt 1999, p. 98).

Lazzarato (2006) is concerned with the almost instant commodification of communication at the heart of immaterial production, where production is camouflaged given the absence of the factory walls, as innately human qualities are woven into the culture of the product. This is expressed in the author's caution to *immaterial labourers* of over-exposing their subjectivities, and the resources of their mind, for their employers to have endless access to. As he explains, "immaterial workers (those who work in advertising, fashion, marketing, television, cybernetics, and so forth) satisfy a demand by the consumer and at the same time establish that demand" (Lazzarato 2006, p. 142). In this sense, creativity should not be perceived as one's expression of individuality that the "superior classes" exclusively enjoy; rather, creativity should be seen as the coming together of many common individualities that "establish that demand" (Lazzarato 2006, p. 142). Immaterial production relies substantially on various material apparatuses in its production of subjectivity—like language, information, and feelings—it is, as such, comprised of new knowledges; immaterial production is what Foucault (1990) describes as a *dispositif* (Hardt & Negri 2009). Thus, "altermodernity provides a strong notion of new values, new knowledges, and new practices; in short, altermodernity constitutes a *dispositif* for the production of subjectivity" (Hardt & Negri 2009, p. 115, emphasis in original).

Contemporary production still trades off largely material products, but producers are nevertheless forced into the immaterial paradigm because affect, symbols, discourses, and desires directly produce social relations; use-value *is* life-value (Hardt & Negri 2000). Virno (2007, p. 5), too, reveals the contemporary production of *social relations* (implicit in immaterial production) when he says: "what is learned, carried out, and consumed in the time outside of labor is then utilized in the production of commodities, becomes a part of the use-value of labor power and is computed as a profitable resource". When a barista, for example, is stressed or embarrassed by the growing number of customers surrounding her while they wait for their takeaway coffees to be made, she might make her efforts expressly transparent to agitated customers, so that they can see she is doing her best; a technique she probably learned outside of working at the café. Or, if a bartender is greeting annoying drunk customers at the bar, she may detach from the unpleasant affects that they invoke in her so that she can greet them pleasantly, just like she would approach people at a party or a 'gig'. While a barista functions as the café's symbolic or aesthetic mirror, she is contributing to the café's overall affect on customers; cultural capital that she most likely accumulates outside of the café. In fact, Nicholas Carah's (2013, p. 348) illuminating research into the labour of musicians in Melbourne reveals the fundamental task required of them was not one of generating individual meaning or developing their creative practice;

rather, they were relied upon "to animate and facilitate the generalised circulation of meaning". The author refers to *communicative enclosures* created out of the affective intensity of the brand—that the workers' job was to represent and make emotionally contagious: "regardless of what musicians and their audiences might think the meaning of any particular performance in branded space is, they construct social networks that are visible and accessible to brands" (Carah 2013, p. 349). Acutely sensitive, this research reveals the way the labour of musicians was closely aligned with "more canny, reflexive and cynical forms of identity", by revealing the crux of the musicians' labour, that is, to be emotionally contagious (Carah 2013, p. 365). In other words, the job of the musicians in Carah's (2013) study was to extend and support a brand and cultural narrative more than to actually create and envision new artistic works as *affective labourers*.

Affect: the feelings before emotion

What does it mean 'to affect' and 'be affected', and how is affect different to emotion? Prior to the sociology of emotions, and before the dominance of positivist science more generally, emotions had long been considered of great importance to social constitutions of justice, equality and a 'good life'—like in the seven cardinal sins in early Christian doctrine (Greco & Stenner 2008, p. 13). Sociologically, the study of emotions traces its origins as a crucial part of the early depictions by the 'founding fathers' of social life in the context of the changes brought by industrialisation. Karl Marx (1993) argued that the capitalist mode of production created individual feelings of alienation as workers grew estranged from themselves and their jobs. Emile Durkheim (1995) argued that negative emotions, like self-extinction, in his study on suicide, and positive emotions of collective effervescence and solidarity, in his study of the division of labour, were directly related to the individual's degree of social integration or sense of belonging. Max Weber (2001), too, saw the modern individual as disenchanted and somebody whose heart bureaucracy had almost totally enveloped in its rationalising logic. While the founding fathers of sociology all interrogated the systemic social conditions that generated feelings and emotions as social determinants, Erving Goffman (1959) situated emotions in the social interactions between people in everyday life.

In his seminal work *The Presentation of Self in Everyday Life*, Goffman (1959) describes individuals as constantly having to manoeuvre and perform their selfhood in order to make everyday life decisions and, yet, those decisions are largely governed by the laws of social convention and normalisation. The paradox, in his words, is that "behind many masks and many characters, each performer tends to wear a single look, a naked and unsocialized look, a look of concentration, a look of one who is privately engaged in a difficult, treacherous task" (Goffman 1959, p. 228). Affect is unlike emotion, which denotes *personal* feeling (Deleuze & Guattari 2013). It is "a prepersonal intensity corresponding to the passage from one experiential state of the body to another and implying an augmentation or diminution in that body's capacity to act" (Deleuze and Guattari 2013, p. xiv).

In other words, socially assigned, or qualified, emotion is secondary to the unconscious and unqualified field of emergence that are affects (Massumi 2002). The transience of affect, for Freud (1997), confirms the nature of the unconscious as ultimately unknowable because affects absorb, and are constitutive of, the person's mind—an archive of unconscious experiences. Where emotions are an embodied and intentional state, affects are in a constant state of transformation and becoming, captured in Freud's (1966) idea that "affect acts" (Seigworth & Gregg 2010, p. 2).

In *The Interpretation of Dreams* Freud (1997) posits the feeling of being born as one's first experience of being affected—that being anxiety—and eventually claims it is one's extremely early childhood that reproduces affects, even those that are pre-individual, or prior to conscious understanding. Hence, the author explains "the act of birth, moreover, is the first experience attended by anxiety, and is the source and model of the affect of anxiety" (Freud 1997, p. 263). The individual stores feelings from birth forming *both* highly personalised accounts of their past, as well as pre-individual, or unconscious, feelings of the body in the spur-of-the-moment that emotion then consciously attributes to socially constructed discourses and languages (Matthis 2000). Feelings, in this way, are sediments of what Patricia Clough (2008, p. 48) describes as "matter as incorporeal potential", whereby "as soon as it begins to inform, it dissolves back into complexity across all scales of matter, like quantum effects feeding the indeterminacy appropriate to each scale of matter". As in the anxious feeling of experiencing life out of the womb for the first time—as the unconscious, or pre-individual, beginning of a life of being affected—Massumi (2002) insists on affects as pre-individual, insofar as they will always leave sediments of preconscious activators for subsequent affects to draw from in their reactivation (Freud 1997).

During the 1970s a range of human sciences reengaged with the project of post-structural and deconstructionist philosophy, at about the same time that affect was being reincorporated into the sociological repertoire, with Foucault as a key figure (Clough 2008; Greco & Stenner 2008, pp. 9–10). Many contemporary post-structural theorists since Foucault distance themselves from the scientific determinism and geneticist emphases of the older positivism that had fallen out of favour significantly during the Parsonian era of sociology, beginning in the 1950s. Rather, the new post-structuralism redelivered biology without *determinism*, emphasising energy, patterns, dynamics, and potential (Leys 2011). Significantly influential here is Gilles Deleuze (1994), who understands affect as distinctly *not* referring to personal feeling, but rather to the spectrum of intensity in the passage from one experiential state into another and the resultant change in the body's capacity to act (Massumi 2015). For Deleuze, affects are the confrontations between things—the relations between bodies and objects that go on to compose assemblages, or clusters, of individuals (Seigworth & Gregg 2010, p. 6). Distinguishing emotion from affect is important for Deleuze because, whereas emotion is defined by personal feeling, affect "is this passing of a threshold, seen from the point of view of the change in capacity" (Massumi 2015, p. 17).

Affects are the confrontations between things—the relations between bodies and objects that go on to compose assemblages, or clusters, of individuals

(Seigworth & Gregg 2010, p. 6). In Deleuze's (1994) thinking, they represent a critical point, or what he calls *bifurcation*, where in a split second "a physical system paradoxically embodies multiple and normally mutually exclusive potentials, only one of which is 'selected'" subject to the chaos of every moment (Massumi 1995, p. 93). For example, at the point at which we experience an affect, like the shock evoked by watching television, the body—as a physical system—is forced into selecting one of the different ideas conjured, in order to negotiate with the feeling of shock that it has encountered during that moment. This is why Deleuze (1988) explains transitioning through affects, and into the expression of emotion, as being the birth place of new ideas, because they transform the body's capacity and potential to move in a new direction. In this way, the body's sense of reality relies on forces and collisions with other things, encounters with other bodies and objects: "affect is what activates us, what connects us with others and thereby confronts us with our own limits" (Carnera 2012, pp. 80–81). Whereas emotion is a *qualified* intensity, insofar as it is socially organised into a meaning that is *ascribed to feeling*, affects are a pre-personal intensity, outside the realm of qualification, and deeply embedded in the situation in which they occur (Deleuze 1988; Deleuze 1994; Deleuze & Guattari 2013; Massumi 1995, 2002, 2015; Spinoza 1996).

Spinoza: on desiring pleasure and pain

More than any other, Benedict de Spinoza's (1996) theory of the affects has been developed furthest and informs most work in the field, including the authors I have mentioned above (Hardt 2007, p. ix). Indeed, as Massumi (1995, p. 88) notes, Spinoza is "a formidable philosophical precursor" of "the difference in nature between affect and emotion". For Spinoza, affects are *modifications* of bodies and ideas that are the result of positive and negative encounters with other bodies and objects, which result in changes of the body's determination and power of understanding (Brown & Stenner 2001). So, feelings mark the mind's *determination* to think "this rather than that"; what Massumi (2015, p. 17) describes as "the passing of a threshold" (Spinoza 1996, p. 112). Spinoza (1996) suggests that feelings are a collective structure as opposed to an individual faculty: they require the collaboration of bodies and objects because the potential of the body is defined by its forces of encounter (Brown & Stenner 2001). It is the friction or collision, the points of confrontation between a body and other bodies (or a body and object) that give way to the feeling (Seigworth & Gregg 2010, p. 3). The extent to which these *forces of encounter* influence the person's sense of self is illuminated when the author says: "For all the ideas we have of bodies indicate the actual constitution of our own body more than the nature of the external body" (Spinoza 1996, p. 112).

In his profound text titled *Ethics*, which was written in 1677 and reads like a manual for the affects, Spinoza (1996) explains that desires encapsulate the essence of a person because desire, as a person's conscious appetite, leads the person to endeavour to attain the things that improved their power of understanding;

hence they desire to have it again. Pornography, for example, epitomises this cycle of acquiring relentless pleasure in which one is never entirely satisfied. Or, a pleasurable experience of buying a new brand of ice-cream will likely produce more attempts by the individual to replicate the pleasure of consuming that new brand of ice-cream, and, possibly, that person will become a repeat customer or continue to seek out newer, better, brands. That is, to feel euphoria arouses a movement in the person toward having and keeping the loved thing by the very "nature of desire"—one's conscious and endless acquisition of appetite (Spinoza 1996, p. 113). And conversely, to feel dysphoria or pain arouses a movement to remove or exclude the hated thing. Affects are rendered 'good' and 'bad' as the person is driven to conceive ways to hold onto or detach from the pleasurable or painful affect, and in doing so their desires create and maintain ideologies governing pleasure, pain, and desire (Spinoza 1996; Rocca 2008). This is the point at which emotion imputes ideas of 'good' and 'bad' onto the transformation taking place within the body; emotionality comes in quick succession to the body's feeling. Using the example of ice-cream again, the person might cultivate taste preferences and ideas around what they feel is 'good' and 'bad' ice-cream.

The more a person feels joyfulness, the more they will seek to continue their joyfulness and the abler they will be to adequately place the joyful idea in the epistemological material of ideas and their relationship to other ideas that constitutes their mind (Deleuze 1988). This is because ideas are *adequately* ordered through common notions: how the idea relates to the person's "epistemological fabric of [other] ideas", meaning that finding common notions with others hinges upon one's own experiential depth (Deleuze 1988, pp. 74–75). Spinoza writes "*if things have nothing in common with one another, one of them cannot be the cause of the other*" (1996, p. 3, emphasis in original). When 'positive' and 'negative' affects enhance, or diminish, a person's arrival at pleasure or pain, ideas born out of such feelings will be ordered either *adequately* or *inadequately* (Brown & Stenner 2001). Ideas conjured in the collision between bodies are part and parcel of the context in which affects are received; one of which the person selects (Brown and Stenner 2001; Deleuze 1988).

For an idea to formulate *adequacy*, then, it must be placed "within the series of ideas currently constituting mind" (Brown & Stenner 2001, p. 93). That is, adequate thinking happens when the person reasons with, and reflects on, their past experiences of feeling and nostalgia—what Deleuze (1988, pp. 74–75) describes as "the epistemological material through which the idea refers to other ideas". This means that in order for adequate ideas to formulate, "we need to experiment with our own experience" (Carnera 2012, p. 78). In this sense, joyful and pleasurable feelings are the result of joyful encounters with other things in the past: forces of encounter that increase the person's power to ensure they last and are repeated (Hardt & Negri 2009). Joy affirms the person's understanding; it affirms the mind's power as the body tells it that it feels good (Spinoza 1996). Correspondingly, if a person is affected with dysphoric feelings, the more that person will transition from a greater power of understanding to a lesser and more passive one, based on the *inadequacy* of the idea and subsequent incomprehension of the emotions oriented around sadness and pain (Williams 2007). Rather than using sociological categories like culture and biology to study affects, Spinoza's legacy teaches us to analyse "modifications as expressive of a singular complexity in which all things are gathered and governed" (Brown & Stenner 2001, p. 104; Sharp 2007).

Overview

Melburnians breath hospitality: cafés and bars provide the city with a source of life, or its "symbolic charge", as a notably liveable metropolitan city (O'Connor 2004, p. 145). The affects engendered by venues' atmospheres and their lasting impact differentiate the value of one venue, or product, over another, all of which are competing for delineation in an environment that is saturated with multiple variations on the same material product. Not only does this sell the products, but the *affective labour* being performed goes on to produce and reproduce the cultural and ideological environment (Lazzarato 2006). By ethnographically situating the café and bar culture in Melbourne, the significance of workers themselves being affected in order to generate value in 'hip' economies is exposed. It was the ways in which not only customers but, more pressingly, workers and employers were moved that determined the product's overall value, which I present as three interactional ecologies of transparency, detachment, and ephemerality. These interactional ecologies functioned according to the maximising of transient pleasures and the minimising of pain and, in the process, they produced 'hip' qualities. Transparency, detachment, and ephemerality were outcomes that followed on from ones experiencing the intensities of feeling.

Not only are customers moved by the experience, but, more pressingly, workers and employers, too, are seduced by atmosphere and vulnerable to the impact of 'the moment' to the point where, in fact, nobody is actually in control. Being pleasurably moved in the short term, at work, simultaneously blocked workers from achieving their goals and from seeing a long-term trajectory, while, at the same time, powerfully seducing them with autonomy, creative expression, flexible hours, spontaneous joy, transparency and authenticity in their interactions, thinking in the moment, and being present. If they were moved with joy, they would very likely provide better service and personally invest in the venue and their employer. Stimulated by pleasure, they were empowered to (lucratively) embody the venue's image. Feelings and ecologies of interaction between workers, the spaces, customers, employers, and the brand more generally—the sensory collisions that they encounter and feel—help to determine the overall value generated by these venues well beyond simple monetary terms. 'Affected labourers' are invested 'players' who, along with the *production cultures* and employers, are together responsible for the production of 'hip' and memorable vibes that fuel the *mood economy* (Gregg 2009; Silva 2013). In Chapter 2, I describe the ways that Melburnians are *expected* to embody taken-for-granted knowledge of the 'hip' hospitality code. The broad and unpredictable range of customers' taken-for-granted knowledge, familiarity, and common sense, led the workers to treat their interactional labour temporally—gauging the customer during the initial encounter—in order to deal with the unpredictable assortment of customers, and affects, they were faced with. In fact, it was largely up to the customer to engage with the worker before any attempts at rapport grew and, if the customer didn't engage, then the worker approached them in the same way—producing a kind of inhospitable hospitality, or hipster service. Thinking and feeling on the spot governed much of the mental frameworks of 'affected labourers' in approaching their jobs, and lives.

In Chapter 3, I explore the unpredictability of customers' level of taken-for-granted knowledge, which materialised in an interactional ecology rooted in transparency: where workers explicitly revealed, often parodying, their labour efforts to the customers who didn't engage or demonstrate cultural competence within the venues. Their transparent approach was the outcome of being affected by such an unpredictable patronage; it was a coping technique for dealing with the negative affects aroused by encounters with those that lack common-sense knowledge or display disrespect toward workers. The workers' degree of appreciation and respect for the venue, lifestyle, and customer determined the type of service they gave, their carrying of the brand, and their overall communication of the venue's message. Just as the affective contagion of venues produced transparent interactions, which communicated in an overtly satirical fashion to customers what was actually involved in serving them, the venues, too, as affectively charged spaces, elevated workers by putting them on a sort of visceral mental platform inside the spaces, releasing them from their serious selves. In Chapter 4, I describe a process of embodied elevation that I observed among workers inside the 'hip' atmospheres of the venues, and this elevation moved them to formulate ideas about the nature of things, observe, assert, and detach from seriousness to pastiche their 'self' at work (Spinoza 1996). They drew on their (often vast) archives of past experiences with "shit customers" as a means of detaching from the disproportionately negative feelings they encountered; the customer was not 'always right' (Sam).

In Chapter 5, I explain how, although they seemingly freely detached from negative encounters, which were disproportionately more common from day-to-day, workers were much less equipped to isolate *pleasurable* feelings that had *short-term* outcomes. Short-term joys, like the job's allowance of flexibility, expressing oneself through dress, being on a social platform that freed them up to exteriorise their identity, being paid in cash, not having any ongoing responsibilities at the end of the shift, etc., were largely fulfilled. At the same time, though, almost every worker explained that they were in a career that was never meant to be a career, feeling 'stuck' and seduced by the short-term rewards inherent in the job that came at the expense of their long-term trajectories. Romantically expressing their love and attraction toward the venue where they worked and their employers, many workers sacrificed their long-term desires—such as getting out of the industry altogether—for the ontologically more gripping force of joy in the short term (Spinoza 1996). Most of them personally invested in the venue they worked for, often holding loyal bonds with their employers and the culture of the venue, seeing themselves as lucky to be there. 'Affected labourers' are lucrative assets for employers, inasmuch as, by virtue of being moved by positive and short-term feeling, they are more likely to invest and, ultimately, be better workers.

Reference list

Beck, U 1992, *Risk Society: Towards a New Modernity*, trans. M Ritter, Sage, Los Angeles.
Boltanski, L & Chiapello, E 2007, *The New Spirit of Capitalism*, trans. G Elliot, Verso, New York.
Brown, SD & Stenner, P 2001, 'Being Affected: Spinoza and the Psychology of Emotion', *International Journal of Group Tensions*, vol. 30, no. 1, pp. 81–104.
Carah, N 2013, 'Brand Value: How Affective Labour Helps Create Brands', *Consumption, Markets & Culture*, vol. 17, no. 4, pp. 346–366.
Carnera, A 2012, 'The Affective Turn: The Ambivalence of Biopolitics Within Modern Labour and Management', *Culture and Organization*, vol. 18, no. 1, pp. 69–84.
Clough, PT 2008, 'The Affective Turn', *Theory, Culture & Society*, vol. 25, no. 1, pp. 1–22.
Deleuze, G 1988, *Spinoza: Practical Philosophy*, trans. R Hurley, City Lights, San Francisco.
Deleuze, G 1994, *Difference and Repetition*, trans. P Patton, Columbia University Press, New York.
Deleuze, G & Guattari, F 2013, *A Thousand Plateaus: Capitalism and Schizophrenia*, trans. B Massumi, Bloomsbury, London, New Delhi, New York & Sydney.
Durkheim, E 1995, *The Elementary Forms of Religious Life*, trans. KE Field, Free Press, Florence.
Eden, D 2012, *Autonomy: Capitalism, Class and Politics*, Ashgate, Burlington.
Foucault, M 1990, *The History of Sexuality Volume One: An Introduction*, trans. R Hurley, Vintage Books, New York.
Foucault, M 2003, *Society Must Be Defended: Lectures at the Collège de France, 1975–76*, trans. D Macey, Picador, New York.
Freud, S 1966, *Project for a Scientific Psychology*, trans. and ed. J Strachey, Hogarth, London.
Freud, S 1997, *The Interpretation of Dreams*, trans. AA Brill, Penguin Group, London.
Giddens, A 1991, *Modernity and Self-Identity*, Stanford University Press, Redwood City.
Gill, R & Pratt, A 2008, 'In the Social Factory? Immaterial Labour, Precariousness and Cultural Work', *Theory, Culture & Society*, vol. 25, no. 7–8, pp. 1–30.
Goffman, E 1959, *The Presentation of Self in Everyday Life*, Cox & Wyman, London.
Greco, M & Stenner, P (eds.) 2008, *Emotions: A Social Science Reader*, Routledge, London & New York, pp. 1–22.
Gregg, M 2009, 'Learning to (Love) Labour: Production Cultures and The Affective Turn', *Communication and Critical/Cultural Studies*, vol. 6, no. 2, pp. 209–214.
Gregg, M 2011, *Work's Intimacy*, Polity, Cambridge & Malden.

Hardt, M 1999, 'Affective Labor', *boundary 2*, vol. 26, no. 2, pp. 89–100.

Hardt, M 2007, 'What Affects Are Good For', *The Affective Turn: Theorizing the Social*, eds. PT Clough & J Halley, Duke University Press, Durham and London.

Hardt, M & Negri, A 2000, *Empire*, Harvard University Press, Cambridge.

Hardt, M & Negri, A 2004, *Multitude: War and Democracy in the Age of Empire*, Penguin Press, New York.

Hardt, M & Negri, A 2009, *Commonwealth*, Belknap Press of Harvard University Press, Cambridge.

Hochschild, AR 1983, *The Managed Heart: Commercialization of Human Feeling*, University of California Press, Berkeley & Los Angeles.

Lasch, C 1979, *The Culture of Narcissism: American Life in an Age of Diminishing Expectations*, George J. McLeod, Toronto.

Lazzarato, M 2006, 'Immaterial Labor', trans. P Colilli & E Emory in *Radical Thought in Italy: A Potential Politics*, eds. M Hardt & P Virno, University of Minnesota Press, Minneapolis, pp. 132–147.

Leys, R 2011, 'The Turn to Affect: A Critique', *Critical Inquiry*, vol. 37, no. 3, pp. 434–472.

Lloyd, A 2012, 'Working to Live, Not Living to Work: Work, Leisure and Youth Identity Among Call Centre Workers in North East England', *Current Sociology*, vol. 60, no. 5, pp. 619–635.

Lyotard, J-F 1984, *The Postmodern Condition: A Report on Knowledge*, University of Minnesota Press, Minneapolis.

Marx, K 1993, *Grundrisse: Foundation of the Critique of Political Economy*, trans. M Nicolaus, Penguin Group, London.

Massumi, B 1995, 'The Autonomy of Affect', *Cultural Critique*, Spring, no. 31, pp. 83–109.

Massumi, B 2002, *Parables for the Virtual*, Duke University Press, Durham & London.

Massumi, B 2015, *The Politics of Affect*, Polity, Cambridge, Oxford & Boston.

Matthis, I 2000, 'Sketch for a Metapsychology of Affect', *International Journal of Psycho-Analysis*, vol. 81, no. 2, pp. 215–227.

May, V 2011, 'Self, Belonging, and Social Change', *Sociology*, vol. 45, no. 3, pp. 363–378.

O'Connor, J 2004, 'A Special Kind of City Knowledge: Innovative Clusters, Tacit Knowledge, and the "Creative City"', *Media International Australia*, vol. 112, pp. 131–149.

Rocca, MD 2008, *Spinoza*, Routledge, New York.

Schutz, A 1953, 'Common-Sense and Scientific Interpretation of Human Action', *Philosophy and Phenomenological Research*, vol. 14, no. 1, pp. 1–38.

Seigworth, GJ & Gregg, M (eds.) 2010, 'An Inventory of Shimmers', *The Affect Theory Reader*, Duke University Press, Durham & London, pp. 1–25.

Sennett, R 1998, *The Corrosion of Character: The Personal Consequences of Work in the New Capitalism*, WW Norton & Company, New York.

Sharp, H 2007, 'The Force of Ideas in Spinoza', *Political Theory*, vol. 35, no. 6, pp. 732–755.

Silva, J 2013, *Coming Up Short: Working-Class Adulthood in an Age of Uncertainty*, Oxford University Press, New York.

Spinoza, B 1996, *The Ethics*, trans. E Curley, Penguin Group, London.

Tsianos, V & Papadopoulos, D 2006, 'Precarity: A Savage Journey to the Heart of Embodied Capitalism', *Transversal Journal*. Available from: http://eipcp.net/transversal/1106/tsianospapadopoulos/en [29 July 2014].

Virno, P 2004, *The Grammar of the Multitude: For an Analysis of Contemporary Forms of Life*, MIT Press, Cambridge & London.

Virno, P 2007, 'General Intellect', *Historical Materialism*, vol. 15, no. 3, pp. 3–8.

Weber, M 2001, *The Protestant Ethic and the Spirit of Capitalism*, trans. T Parsons, Routledge, New York.

Williams, C 2007, 'Thinking the Political in the Wake of Spinoza: Power, Affect and Imagination in the Ethics', *Contemporary Political Theory*, vol. 6, no. 3, pp. 349–369.

2 Melbourne's affect

The production of a 'hip' industry

'Melbourne-style' cafés

Melbourne is internationally renowned for its café and bar culture contributing to its global liveability standard, as well as its celebration of street laneways, graffiti, and possibly even its cycling culture, too. Hospitality is embedded in the culture of the city. The market is saturated with bars and cafés offering the same arbitrary product: coffee and alcohol. Together, the atmosphere, production culture, worker, and user are involved in the ideological enlargement of the product—what it communicates and what it represents (Gregg 2009; Lazzarato 2006). "It's arguably the highest coffee culture in the world," proclaimed Jess, a capable yet slightly disenchanted young waitress who works at a café in Northcote—a gentrified inner northern suburb in Melbourne that is populated with second-hand clothing and book shops, organic grocers, superfood cafés, and 'grunge' countercultural pubs that predate the suburb's gentrification. We enjoyed a beer together at a bar across the road from where she worked, after her shift, along with Tim, another young male worker who possessed a similarly uncanny wit, and together they indulged me in a conversation built largely around their anecdotal social pessimism toward café patrons and the lack of common decency shown by customers. Both Tim and Jess had pursued academic study, and yet, like so many other workers I spoke with, they found themselves still serving people despite the array of problems they saw so clearly in their vocational reality. Early in our interview, Jess gave me a biographical vignette of her work history, which was hospitality-oriented, though she had not intended it to be so. She told me she had recently lived in New York and made coffee there. Reflecting on her observations of how Melbourne's cafés compared on an international metropolitan scale, Jess said:

> So, like, in New York there's like maybe, now, Bluestone where I worked, and they were the first to do it well. 'Melbourne-style cafés' is literally what it says on their business cards. 'Melbourne-style coffee shop', because 'Melbourne-style' is like a genre of café, and basically all that boils down to is good coffee, as opposed to what else is on the market in New York. It's not good coffee, it's not espresso, it's all drip or whatever. So yeah there's

a lot of hype associated with it. At Bluestone you would get served a coffee with a basic love heart in it and when you put it down on the table people go ballistic, whereas in Melbourne if you get served a coffee with a love heart on you think this person doesn't know what they're doing.

During another evening, I sat drinking a cocktail in an old dark cocktail bar right in the centre of the city, its exposed bricks painted black. As I walked up the many flights of industrial stairs to get to the bar, I was greeted by three male bartenders—all wearing black waistcoats, black pants, and white shirts, carrying a proud posture. The atmosphere of the bar felt curiously 'old world' compared with the other bars I had visited in Melbourne: soft jazz music was playing, candles were the primary source of lighting, and customers always seemed to whisper quietly as they hunched over their lounge chairs and vintage-sewing-machine tables. Throughout the evening, I chatted informally over the bar with Arthur, who I later interviewed. He, too, was quick to de-familiarise the hospitality culture in Melbourne, possibly prompted by his moving over from Norway some two years ago. "For a city of four million there's a lot going on!" he called out to me from across the bar as he proudly polished cocktail glasses during downtime. He focused his eyes back on the glass that was in his hand, for a moment's solitude, before calling back with sharp eye contact from across the bar: "Massive coffee culture and the massive breakfast culture, all-day breakfast culture, I've never seen it anywhere else. I saw an article in the *New York Times* that said it was the biggest breakfast culture in the world!" Indeed, there is a distinctiveness about the industry in Melbourne: the all-day breakfast culture, or the fact that "a basic love heart" latte art is considered amateurish. In fact, at the café I worked in as I began this research, we were all expected to pour steamed milk into the shape of tulip flowers with at least six to nine separate 'leaves'. We learned this through militant repetition and compulsory training sessions, given by the company's best baristas at their coffee roasting site.

Part of the intensity of competition in Melbourne's café and bar industry, and the saturated hospitality market, is the very rapid development of high-density living in Melbourne's inner northern suburbs, where gentrification has intensified and property is becoming increasingly commercialised and thus unaffordable (Lobato 2006). This means that property developers provide "fantasies of inner-urban bohemia" for investors, professionals, and retirees to purchase, and, in doing so, shift and sculpt the cultural and ideological geography of the city (Lobato 2006, p. 67). For example, where the bayside suburb of St Kilda was "formerly a haven for artists and musicians", it is "now a magnet for property developers", leaving many disadvantaged groups squeezed out through these processes of gentrification to other areas of the city and suburbia (Lobato 2006, p. 67). While commercialisation and gentrification may provide economic advantages for hospitality inasmuch as urban density increases street traffic and thus improves sales, it also means that an overwhelming number of venues open and close shortly thereafter because of extensive product competition, effectively pricing the venues out of the market. In fact, the commercialisation of historically affordable, working-class, inner suburbs like Brunswick, Collingwood, Fitzroy, and Northcote seemed marked when I was in venues that were clearly distinguishing themselves from the flow of gentrified ideologies governing the aesthetics and ethics of the suburbs, as was communicated in the venues' atmosphere. One of the cafés, for example, in Fitzroy—which is a rapidly gentrifying area—communicated an ethical aesthetical message incongruous with the host of newer venues that represent Fitzroy's mainstream commercial agenda in 2018. Where most new venues on the same street are trendy and clean, often featuring state-of-the-art coffee machines and/or artisanal breakfast food, this venue communicated countercultural ideas, glorifying mess and promoting a 'be yourself' attitude. In fact, the venue is one of the oldest bars in Melbourne and, according to the manager, is therefore able to retain its identity amidst the changing suburban psychogeography of Melbourne today. In this way, hospitality is emblematic of the gentrification process.

I met the manager of this café and bar in Fitzroy at the end of the day after her shift, and we had a beer in the venue's courtyard while it slowly got more and more rowdy, making it difficult to hear each other. Stacy seemed to represent the aesthetical messages of the venue perfectly: pink hair, rainbow-patterned knee-high socks, platform sneakers, and hair ties that were shaped like little bones—like the character, Pebbles, from *The Flintstones*. She often gave me free or discounted drinks while I was observing or interviewing, and embodied a casual and open-minded disposition and was fondly known, by name, by all of the venue's regular customers and product stockists. During our beer, Stacy told me about the explicit requirement of venues creating a memorable experience, based on the current environment—the overabundance of hospitality. She explained the centrality of venues being unique—like the venue she managed—in order to stand out. Based on the sheer volume of hospitality venues in the city, Stacy explained: "Like someone could be like, 'I work at this café', you'll be like, 'Oh, I don't even know where that is'—you know?" She went on to point out that they are able to skirt around advertising the venue, because they are so well established, having developed a reputation based on its age:

> People just kind of know of it through the years. Whereas other places I go to you could be like, 'Oh yeah, that was a nice breakfast nice place,' but, wash over and then it just becomes another café. It's got be something that stands out to make you go back there, or something.

The endless refinement involved in standing out from the crowd is characteristic of the broader contemporary production context that commodifies the resources of the mind through immaterial production (Hardt & Negri 2000).

Barney, who worked in the 'old-world' cocktail bar in the centre of the city, told me that most Australian drinkers are hesitant to try new drinks, but that is exactly what the industry is all about. While the product has remained the same in basic properties inasmuch as coffee is coffee and beer is beer, it is the refinement of the product and the culture around espresso and cocktails that, following Arthur, is the motor of the industry. At the same venue, when I sat down and spoke with another bartender, named Johnny, who had moved to Melbourne from New Zealand some ten years ago, he expressed the level at which he thought Melbourne hospitality operated on, breeding competition, innovation, and endless product refinement, resulting in extremely high quality and overall standards. It is the standard of service that strikes Johnny as distinctive, in the sense that even "at your shitty café in the suburbs, if you're not greeted well at the door and get water and just like all of that shit is just absolute", when in an international context such detail would be "rare". He went on to suggest, as we sat in the massive antique armchairs at the venue while it was empty and his shift had yet to begin, that such a process of refinement breeds innovation because businesses are always looking for the next thing for the sole purpose of setting themselves apart from the rest. So that, "if you're not at that level you won't get people through the door" (Johnny).

The endlessness of immaterial products' refinement, which Johnny framed in terms of "innovation" happens because, like many immaterial and service-based commodities, cafés and bars are a "nonessential industry" (Zippy—the second-in-charge bartender in a Collingwood bar). Compared with, for example, teachers, doctors, lawyers, or those holding professional status more generally, the job of baristas and bartenders is to fulfil desires more than immediate needs (Zippy). As Zippy put it: "It's like a nonessential industry. It's not other jobs. If you're a doctor or an accountant or whatever, you're needed." Drawing a distinction between needs- and wants-based products, she explained the way the labour she does is predicated on this distinction: that rather than people needing them, "with hospitality people come to you when they want to" (Zippy). The venue's nonessential status is perhaps why Aroha, too, explained her perspective of competitive hospitality in Melbourne as "making these people believe in what we're doing and come back", given they do not necessarily need to. Zara, whose job it was to greet all incoming customers at the café's front door, which was off a thin, graffiti-clad, laneway in South Melbourne that, like many venues, one would struggle to find if one wasn't really looking, explained: "You can see people leave that have had that and they've paid, like, fucking one hundred dollars for breakfast for two people, and they've been kicked out after 45 minutes and they're still like, 'Wow!'" Immaterial surplus, in the form of the reaction venues engender, and the workers' strength at communicating the product's representation and message, are decisive in immaterial markets catering to fruitful wants and desires.

My first and freest interview during the research was with the manager of a café in Collingwood who, toward the end of the interview, having conversed with me so generously while eating delivered pizza and counting the till for the day, shared some of his predictions for the hospitality culture in Melbourne. He told me that with so many new venues opening up, there is still the same amount of people in Melbourne, which he believes will engender "a wacky shift over the next few years, depending on what we're serving and the prices of the items" (Jasper). I asked him to elaborate on what he meant by this and he explained that "there's some really talented people doing some really talented stuff", and that those "dodgy cafés in Melbourne" will eventually run out of business, the more that new places open up and the less affordable that hospitality becomes (Jasper). He went on to use a pertinent analogy to communicate the level of competition and product refinement involved in staying alive in the industry. He described how if one isn't improving their venue it is inevitably "going downhill. That's the rule . . . well, if you're not working on going forward, then you're going to go backwards. It's like a treadmill: if you don't keep running you're going to fall off!" (Jasper). That immaterial production is like running on a treadmill that never stops means that, for example, a cup of coffee can, over ten or fifteen years, be transformed into a symbolic metropolitan symbol. One that, in its approximate $3.50, covers ethically sensible production, refined taste profiles, the adoption of new product rhetoric and jargon, an attitudinal and affective character, refined and multiplied methods of executing that cup of coffee, and an overwhelming multiplication of spaces opening up in the city to accommodate and provide the desirable aesthetic with which the cup of coffee is associated.

The impact of techno-capitalism, and particularly social media and communication technologies, on the immaterial production is driven by what Gregg (2009) usefully describes as *production cultures*, where both labourer and consumer are collectively involved in shaping the direction of the product. This, she says, is exemplified in academia, where the *affective labourer*'s deep attachment to work, described as *sacrificial labour*, helps to create the ideological environment for the consumers of the product provided—the students. Thus, the author reflects: "The potential for academic production cultures to perpetuate a destructive combination of workaholism, frequent flyer lifestyles, and constant connectivity has been at the forefront of my thinking" (Gregg 2009, p. 212). Gregg (2009, p. 212) advises that, if academics themselves are to recognise the "peculiarity" of their *production cultures*, they will likely only be able to do this by thinking outside "the present" demands of an exhausting schedule requiring their constant connectivity. What the author also crucially highlights is that such deep attachments in the *sacrificial labour* performed by the workers are indeed unpaid and conducted relatively autonomously by the worker. Yet striving for such things provides precisely the *immaterial labourer*—as an academic in Gregg's (2009) case—with wellbeing and enhanced productivity, and ultimately makes their job more enjoyable, in light of the increasing productivity pressures and demands facing a variety of contemporary workers.

Social media, especially, democratises modes of expression enabling people to exteriorise their identity, while, at the same time, it is a lucrative marketing platform in which venues, patrons, and workers participate and create the *production culture* (Gregg 2009; Hardt & Negri 2000). Hospitality venues function in the same way—with artisanal websites and social media profiles. I was also to learn early on in the field that ratings and reviews and even comments sections on internet websites, or more commonly upmarket 'hip' and up-to-date Melbourne lifestyle websites like Broadsheet, or Three Thousand, are relied on substantially, and that negative reviews are damaging indeed. Jess explained this in terms of the venue having prestige and being well known, like the venue she worked at, in the sense that it will generate value "if it's a place that people feel a little privileged to go and have breakfast". During fieldwork, I spent a portion of each week scrolling through the affective goldmine of the internet and, on one of those days, I saw an advertisement pop up on the Facebook homepage. It read: "A new breakfast spot is enough of a reason to meet up with an old friend," and pictured two young, joyful, café-goers deep in conversation, sitting in a well-affected café space, complete with exposed brick, mismatching crockery, indoor plants, and so on. The image was also solidified with golden lighting and a colour overlay screaming of the old-meets-new pastiche, characteristic of popular postmodern affects (Jameson 1998). The image stood out for me as symbolic of the general other-worldliness of café and bar spaces in Melbourne, and their functioning affectively as social lubricators or enablers. Epitomised by the advertisement's positioning of 'the new breakfast spot', rather than the strength of a human bond as *the* decisive factor in choosing to meet up with an old friend, the image said a lot about the affect of hospitality in today's metropolis.

Such *production cultures*, where workers, consumers, fans, and owners alike are increasingly integrated into the productive process, shaping and directing it, provides the city with—borrowing from Justin O'Connor (2004, p. 145)—its "symbolic charge". Mirroring Gregg's (2009) analysis, O'Connor says:

> Signs are plugged into global circuits; the local culture transforms these into something unique and thus able to be re-sent out into the world. Crucially this local culture is that of the city, the vibrant metropolis. This is the crucible where innovative consumption meets ear-to-the-ground production; where the ideas, skills, rivalry, part-time jobs, support networks and distribution outlets of the 'innovative milieu', the 'art world', the 'creative field', come together.
>
> (2004, p. 134)

Melburnians breathe hospitality. Cafés and bars make up a significant aspect of Melbourne's culture and, as such, constitute an increasingly competitive market that is dependent upon affect in its constant requirement of aesthetic and ethical reimagining of a 'nonessential' product (Zippy). The gentrification of urban Melbourne contributes to the saturated market, as increasingly more new venues come and go, in accord with the intense product competition, pricing the venues out of the market. The ideological enlargement of 'hip' Melbourne cafés and bars extends beyond the commodity transaction, into the dialect and popular culture of the city more broadly. It is in this way that cafés and bars in Melbourne are what Foucault (1990) terms a *dispositif*—or apparatus—"for the production of subjectivities" (Hardt & Negri 2009, p. 113).

Common-sense knowledge in 'hip' spaces

One evening midweek, during a quiet service at the three-storey candlelit bar downtown, and I was at one of two occupied sewing-machine tables at this point, the barman, after looking like he had been pondering over something during the time it took to slice all the lemons, looked up and said, "Imagine if you shut down hospitality for a day! It's an incredibly important industry for what it can offer, but people aren't respected for doing it, because, apparently, anyone can do it" (Barney). As we continued our informal conversation over the bar, while Barney found odd jobs to do, my awareness grew of the general expectation within the industry that Melburnians were expected to know the trade through being the, possibly, daily patrons of a saturated and wants-based market. Like Rose, the manager from a café in Fitzroy that was an old converted cottage, said: "We all do it: we all go out." The expectation that Melburnians should know the industry, on a much deeper level than most services, was illuminated by the overwhelming assortment of *customers* that initiated the till interaction by asking "How are you?" before anything else. I noticed early in my observations the loudness of customers' efforts to relate to workers, much more than the other way around, in a pantomime dynamic that David Bell (2011) describes as *hostguesting*, where host and guest roles intermingle and blur. Part of this role reversal, or *hostguesting*, is attributable to the embeddedness of hospitality and its latent place in everyday life, which Gregg (2009) synthesises as part of the broader *production cultures* essential to immaterial production (Bell 2011). Particularly online, in such mediums as user-generated knowledge, rating and review platforms, chat groups, comments sections, social media, and so forth, hosts and guests alike actively contribute toward the production of the overall product, sculpting its movement (Gregg 2009). Moreover, by the market dancing with and reacting to the consumer and vice versa, the productive sequence becomes less and less predictable. This way, the market can account for the unpredictability of reactions, trends, and affects, out of which the products derive their value.

Much everyday conversation in Melbourne is anchored by hospitality, and the affects provoked by such experiences; city-goers are constantly rating and reflecting on their experiences of dining out and drinking. I watched a thrilled customer one evening tell the barman about a recent experience that he had at a bar, and the barman was quick to reply, "Did they treat you well there?" A customer, at one point, came and cheerfully greeted the barista from the other side of the coffee machine. She popped her head over the cups stacked on top of the machine and said, "You're on the bus today!" I had heard the term 'bus' (an industry nickname for the coffee machine) during my time working at the specialty coffee shop in central Melbourne. In fact, I learned many new industry terms working in Melbourne, like the 'magic', which refers to a double shot of espresso filled up with steamed milk. Whereas in New Zealand, in the cafés in which I had worked, a 'magic' was referred to as a 'flat white' (with a double shot of espresso, anyway). So, the new forms of knowledge, subjectivities, and terminology, born out of café and bar venues, reflect the taken-for-granted knowledge that workers expect one should know as a customer in the space. This generation and circulation of new languages reiterates Hardt's (1999, p. 98) point—that immaterial commodities "are a form-of-life".

Hospitality is especially lived by way of its centrality to private and public sociality. Like Rose sharply put it, "We all do it: we all go out." This was illuminated in the importance almost all workers placed on common-sense knowledge, espe-cially given the anthropology of hospitality; we all do it (Rose). Jürgen Habermas (1991) traces coffee houses and salons, grounded in the 19th-century city, as crucial predecessors of the public sphere across Europe, primarily through their instigation of civilised public discourse. Despite processes of bureaucratisation evident during this period, it was the critical discussion and rational arguments happening within coffee houses and salons that provided the greatest insight for his influential portrait of the public sphere (Felton 2012). Certainly, in this research, customers were largely expected to know the trade through being the doers and receivers of hospitality in everyday life, both at home and in the public sphere. But the common sense required of café- and bar-goers in Melbourne was a spectrum of taken-for-granted knowledge, insofar as the range of people's under-standings of industry standards spanned far and wide. On the one hand, I watched a fair amount of familiar behaviour, in the sense that customers demonstrated their knowledge of the industry by embodying and identifying with the venue. For example, some customers would ask for a 'magic', rather than a flat white, the former industry nickname, which when uttered in the café communicated one's industry or *insider* knowledge. Or some customers would ask if there were any daily 'specials' on offer, and, in doing so, demonstrated their understanding of hospitality systems and ways of offering the product. Or customers asked what the bartender recommended they drink, communicating their trust and respect for him or her. The taken-for-granted knowledge of hospitality reflects its latent place in the everyday life of urban culture.

On the other hand, the *range* of taken-for-granted knowledge was reinforced as I watched and, at times, was guilty myself of vacant and thoughtless behaviour, thus signalling to workers my own lack of taken-for-granted knowledge or *out-sider* knowledge. I arrived at the bar in Collingwood early one afternoon before it had opened to interview the manager, Jack, who was on his laptop and drinking a beer as I entered. The bar was dark, chairs were stacked on tables, it was silent, and it felt disappointing to see it so void of atmosphere. Jack offered me a drink before we began our interview and, in my mind, because I was in a cocktail bar that sold a lot of whisky, I asked for a whisky sour, which is a moderately technical and, perhaps in hindsight, an annoying drink to make. I reflected, after Jack said, "Could you just have a beer?", that I should refrain from assuming bartenders to be eager and hanging out to make a cocktail. Rather, he wanted simply to pour me a pint of beer. So, in this particular sequence I was the 'them' to the 'us'. But, more generally, across venues, customers would often pour through the door with an expectant forcefulness, which frustrated workers who in many ways expressed custodial body language. In fact, on one occasion, I watched a customer enter the café, ignoring the 'Please wait' sign at the door. She proceeded to point to the table she wanted to sit down at before she took the seat. A new customer pushed in front of her and sat down, and the waitress said, "OK, I'll find somewhere else for you to sit then," before the *customer directed the waitress* where she wanted to sit. Such examples reflect the spectrum of taken-for-granted knowledge that the patrons possess and that workers deal with on a daily basis.

At the same café in South Melbourne, on the table next to mine, I overheard a customer order a cold soy latte, and the waitress paused and half-heartedly nodded, "Yep, I'll see if we've got soy," before the customer quickly replied, "You usually do!" And, when a customer approached the till of the café in Fitzroy, Rose was in the middle of steaming milk, and was the only worker able to serve. Nevertheless, the customer immediately launched ahead, without reserve, and demanded, "Can I pay for the salmon bagel and bacon sandwich?" But, when another member of the same group came in to pay their bill, the customer began by saying, "Thanks a lot for doing that," presumably because she had seen Rose split the bill for the previous customer, who was also part of their group. Having observed so many till interactions by this stage in the fieldwork, I realised the degree to which something as simple as the common question "Can we pay separately?" operationalises the customer's acknowledgement of industry systems and protocols. This is because split bills are often loathed by staff and, as such, will often be refused or ruminated over after closing time. Similarly, I overheard another customer at a café ask, of her own accord, "Do you have any specials?" and, in doing so, was indicating her expectation of similar products and systems being on offer across café venues. There was a range of taken-for-granted industry knowledge—workers were constantly dealing with both unfamiliar and sometimes even disrespectful customers, as well as understanding ones who were familiar with hospitality protocols. This is perhaps why Zippy explained that seeing "all colours of humanity" in the patronage of the bar could be such an unpredictable and potentially disturbing experience. Like she said, "You really do see it all" (Zippy).

It became ever more noticeable how each venue's atmospheric affects aligned with their ethics of service, and this was made especially clear in numerous venues, across different suburbs, during the same day. Following Massumi (2002), affects work on sensations, atmospheres, and what many workers in the venues described as 'the vibe'. Therefore, looking through the lens of affect illuminates the force of visceral and sensory elements of the social, which, as I have noted, are crucial to generating surplus value in the contemporary economy, as well as informing liberal market governance or laissez-faire capitalism. This recalls the idea that immaterial products generate surplus from the products' ideological enlargement: what it means and what it represents (Lazzarato 2006). To put it differently, the material products are the same, but their ideological and affective values differentiate them. Across venues, atmosphere and vibe were clearly reified, and, perhaps more importantly, became a vehicle for instituting ethics and the products' ideological enlargement more generally. The Northcote café, for example, though it never directly stated it, seemed to specialise in purity and newer takes on 'good health', with products ranging from kale and avocado smoothies to its popular nutrient-rich salad. Each time I visited this café it seemed to be busy; its healthful organic salad was a constant sell-out and the clientele demographics appeared largely consistent with the aesthetical ethics of the venue—'hip' young professionals and families who were presumably appreciative of, and could afford, organic ingredients, newly discovered health food, a place to put their pram, or the minimalist design, etc. Workers in this venue were especially muted in their styles of service, and the business was run by a seemingly wealthy family who would often use the café as a meeting point for the family to gather. They would sit together over one of the (always busy) café's prime tables, with their children and children's children, casually eating, drinking, and observing their space, while two of the family members—the sons of the owners—served customers. The family helped to set the scene, if you like.

The café and bar in Fitzroy that I mentioned earlier as glorifying mess, on the other hand, had ripped couches scattered across the floor, a turntable, graffiti-painted walls both inside and out, plants hanging from the ceiling, psychedelic artworks sold on behalf of local artists, and dank odorous toilets. I would meet all sorts of characters during my time in this venue: homeless people, travellers, young artists with hospitality jobs on the side, and, once, an ex-junkie who pulled his dog into the courtyard in a handmade carriage. What I am saying is that the atmosphere was affective and became ethical through the products' ideological enlargement—that is, in terms of what it communicated and represented. Moreover, it was the affects and the products' ideological messages that organised and filtered behaviour within the spaces, by encouraging customers to fit in to the vibe of the venue. And when I spoke to the manager of this venue, she outwardly said, "We hire if the person fits" (Stacy). So much so that the distinctive characters who made up the clientele of each venue actually mirrored the ethics and styles of service specific to each place, like the venues I described above.

The range of common-sense knowledge among the patronage of each venue strengthened the division between insider and outsider, or what many staff described in terms of 'us and them', and, in doing so, filtered and ethicised behaviour in the spaces. Workers expressed clear expectations around what customers should feel, and with whom that feeling should be felt—the phenomenon that Hochschild (1983) conceptualises as *feeling rules*. They desired that their customers adhere to the *feeling rules* and behavioural codes of the venue, and its ethical and aesthetical messages, which workers embodied and conveyed according to the customers' degree of taken-for-granted knowledge. For example, "manners, knowing when or how to order a drink, how to talk to a barman or waitress" became central levers in the workers' gauging of customers' familiarity with the space (Zippy). In fact, it was the customers' ability to gauge the *feeling rules* of the venue, and industry more broadly, that created the 'us and them' mentality to which so many workers referred (Hochschild 1983). Zippy explicitly told me that one develops an unconscious 'us versus them' mentality as a coping mechanism, when confronted with people who have never worked a day in hospitality in their life and struggle with things like manners, knowing when or how to order a drink, and how to talk to a barman or waitress. She even said, "You can tell the people who come in and have never before worked in hospitality because they hold themselves a different way" (Zippy). Since Zippy has been working in hospitality, she tells me, whenever she goes out herself, she now treats her waitresses and bartenders in a different way because she knows how they feel and what they've been through.

The embeddedness of cafés and bars means Melburnians are expected to know the trade through being the daily patrons of a saturated and wants-based market. Melburnians are constantly describing, rating, and reflecting on their experiences of hospitality, making it embedded in the culture of the city. This was reflected in workers' expectations that customers would possess adequate taken-for-granted knowledge, or common-sense knowledge such as not splitting bills, waiting at the right end of the till line, using the industry terminology, or presenting an identifiable cultural symbol. Furthermore, the expectation of taken-for-granted knowledge was the basis of the 'us and them' mentality expressed by many workers, which curated and reflected the patronage of each venue.

Unpredictability and production in 'the moment'

Workers are forced into managing transactional relationships *on a case-by-case basis*, based on the customers' display of taken-for-granted knowledge and adherence to the *feeling rules* of the space at the time of the encounter (Hochschild 1983). The on-the-spot decision-making and on-the-spot thinking required of the workers fits within the temporalities of *disruption culture*, more generally, and precarious contemporary labour-market conditions, comprised of casual workers who have not signed formal contracts, are often paid cash 'under the table' as wages—so that companies avoid paying certain taxes and superannuation—as well as the nonstandard, or flexible, hours that employees are required to work, expressed in the casualisation of many industries (Sennett 1998; Snyder 2016). Personally, I was denied my accumulated superannuation savings when I left my café job, despite my efforts to seek remuneration, and I did not receive even one day of paid sick or holiday leave. This is part of what Autonomist Marxist scholars understand as the "temporality of life" becoming "governed by work" in the immaterial production paradigm, or *precariousness*: the general state of uncertainly and instability felt by a diverse range of workers, irrespective of the status or class category they might fit into (Gill & Pratt 2008, p. 17).

Frequently, staff told me that each day is never the same; indeed, much of their job is to think and move according to a largely unpredictable and precarious time frame, governed by reaction and the momentariness of forces of encounter, or affect. After sitting down at the modern superfood café in Northcote one afternoon, I greeted the manager before he took my coffee order. He told me that he was ready for bed because he had trained a new employee in the morning and the café was quiet, which paradoxically "makes things harder" (George). "That's when things go wrong," he said, because when it is quiet staff become too relaxed and careless, lacking the alertness born out of a chaotic and unpredictably busy café or bar (George). When it was busy, workers were forced into alertness and into thinking on the spot, being faced with multiplying potential and unpredictable encounters with customers, as opposed to when it was quiet—then the job was more predictable and workers were not stimulated by the variability of affects. The present mindset required of workers actually enabled their dealing with the unpredictability implicit in service work.

The temporal and precarious mindset required of the *affective labourer* is described well by Sennett (1998) as flexibility. In his seminal work *The Corrosion of Character: The Personal Consequences of Work in the New Capitalism*, the author explains that while many theorists claim routine is fading away, most labour remains Fordist in principle, only now it is couched in terms like 'flexibility'. This flexibility, Sennett (1998) explains, is required of today's contemporary workers, both in terms of their geographic mobility as well as their working hours, practices, and casualised or informal contracts. For Hardt (1999), immaterial production has moved into a newer phase of *Toyota-ism*, which is based on the conversation between markets and consumers, and vice versa, where stock levels are kept low and productive decisions tend to be made a lot less in advance—they are made in 'the moment'. In the café and bar venues, for example, menus were designed with less solidity, longevity, and formality than one might think, and simplified logos were commonly used to eliminate other symbols in the design process and thus avoid waste and printing and design costs associated with making weekly amendments to the products the venues offered. Similarly, cheap paper was commonly used for printing menus, often displayed on clip boards, in the knowledge that they would be removed and reprinted with next week's selection of, for example, single-origin coffee on offer. In other words, stock levels were kept low so that produce could be local and therefore fresh, seasonal, and more ecologically sound, by eliminating excess waste, and hence enhancing cost efficiencies.

But the time consciousness, according to which cafés and bars operated, was paradoxically situated within a rigid, and even, at times, militant, structure of discipline and rules. Jane described the repetition in terms of, "When it's busy you know it's like, 'Hi, how's it going, here's your menus, these are the specials, can I get you a drink to start?' like, a hundred times, which I don't really like." I was personally confronted with this militarisation, for example, during my time working in the specialty espresso bar in Melbourne's city centre ('the CBD'). The insistence of my manager and co-workers on meticulously folding the Chux cleaning cloths, and the precise repertoires for maintaining at all times perfectly folded, steam-cleaned, stacked cloths in the baristas' section became an obsessive hourly task. Jess, too, from the café in Northcote, found herself in the middle of the job's simultaneous monotony and human spontaneity, saying, "Your role is very monotonous, like day in day out, but I guess every day is different in the human aspect, the varying new jokes, new people to engage with or something, I don't know." For Jess, like many others pointed out, the *human aspect* is what provided variation in the otherwise repetitive, militarised day's work. And when I spoke with Angus, a barman working in the CBD, he pointed out that no matter how repetitive the actual job is, opening beers, running food to tables, and so on, talking to people and interacting with them "is always going to be different". *Toyota-ism* allows room for unpredictability in the productive model by dancing *with* the consumer rather than predicting their course of gratification, yet it also relies on precise systems and militant repetition in order to be flexible (Hardt 1999).

To put it in different terms, it was common for workers to predict a certain number of people they will serve during their shift, and this is reinforced in the monotonous programming of daily tasks. But that predictability, at a certain point, stops, and the affective productive model is largely based on unpredictability, adrenaline, and shakes. For example, a rush might be expected, but it is unknown when it will hit, or a group of people have a lunch booking yet it's unclear as to which 'types' the group will be. This means that the workers' mastery over mundane techniques of the trade is only one side of their working reality, allowing them to deal efficiently with the other side of their working reality: the unpredictable, variable, and possibly irrational encounters that come with any form of service work. So, it is the rigidity of seemingly trivial tasks, like maintaining a routine for folding cloths, or speaking the first verse of the initial encounter—"Hi, how's it going, here's your menus, these are the specials, can I get you a drink to start?"—that allow more freedom and open up the possibility of doing, or not doing, more than just "service with a smile" (Jane). Like resilience is required in *Toyota-ism*, Sennett (1998) insightfully tells us, flexibility refers to a tree's branches and their adaptability to not only sway and bend in various ways but, perhaps more importantly, to spring back into their original form (Hardt 1999). Put differently, the freedom allowed by flexibility comes after its antithesis: swinging back into its original form, which, in the context of production, was achieved by repetitive discipline. Further, what made the job meaningful, affective, and enjoyable was the mastery of rigid and, at times, militant norms of the establishment.

The flexibility required in *Toyota-ism* is part of the hegemony of *immaterial labour*, because workers are simultaneously compelled to strive for wellbeing at work through, for example, flexible working arrangements, while at the same time they are exploited by such autonomous expressions of their deep attachment to the job (Gregg 2009; Hardt 1999; Sennett 1998). The authors describe *affective labour* as living labour precisely because it produces life itself—subjectivities, societies, vibes, discourses, and networks, etc., so that "what is created in the networks of *affective labour* is a form-of-life" (Hardt 1999, p. 98). By living their labour, workers are vulnerable to capital's appropriation of their selfhood, because the products they produce are "a form-of-life", inasmuch as consumers, commentators, critics, workers, and owners all contribute to the production of the product and, in doing so, they sculpt the industry's direction and reproduce 'hipness' (Hardt 1999, p. 98; Gregg 2009). The products of *immaterial labour* powerfully produce and reproduce discourses, societies, needs, images, tastes, and so on, becoming ideological in the process of their commodification and consumption, as affects are rendered 'good' and 'bad' (Rocca 2008; Spinoza 1996). Nicholas Carah (2014, p. 347) puts this well when he says: "Brands do not just attribute a standardised set of qualities to a product or service. Brands are social processes that rely on the participation of consumers and other cultural actors to create value." This renders much of the job of the *affective labourer* to "facilitate the circulation of meaning, identity and social relations" (Carah 2014, p. 347).

In the act of consuming, the products themselves are not destroyed in the sense of, for example, finishing a cup of coffee at a café. Rather, as a result of consuming a cup of coffee in a café, the product is enlarged, transformed, and serves to create the ideological and cultural environment for the consumer and hopefully engage with potential repeat customers who share the experience. Following Lazzarato (2006), instead of the commodity producing the physical capacity of labour power or service, it transforms the person who uses it, and, if it succeeds in doing this, gains use-value or life-value. This is why Lazzarato says:

> Immaterial labor produces first and foremost a 'social relationship' (a relationship of innovation, production, and consumption). Only if it succeeds in this production does its activity have an economic value. This activity makes immediately apparent something that material production had 'hidden', namely, that labor produces not only commodities, but first and foremost it produces the capital relation.
>
> (2006, p. 147, brackets in original)

Because workers face an unpredictable patronage so constantly, as illustrated in the customers' lack of taken-for-granted knowledge reported on by so many workers, they are forced into managing transactional relationships transiently, based on the customers' display of taken-for-granted knowledge and adherence to the *feeling rules* of the space, at the time of encounter (Hochschild 1983). This flexibility is, more generally, a characteristic of postmodern or *Toyota-ist* production under which immaterial surplus thrives (Hardt 1999).

Summary

Past the point of consumer demand, being affected by a memorable experience fuels Melbourne's (hospitality) culture and its ability to generate value and return, as displayed in the overwhelming number of new venues opening up, many of which close down shortly after through being outcompeted, in an accelerating industry. Despite the saturated market, each venue successfully distinguishes itself from its neighbours in an attempt to survive and flourish, in a process of endless product refinement. Based on this intensity of product competition, Melburnians are almost expected to know the trade through being the daily patrons, reflected in the overt displays of *hostguesting*, where host and guest roles collide, eroding the binary between workers and patrons (Bell 2011). The taken-for-granted knowledge that was born out of workers expecting patrons to know the *feeling rules* and common-sense industry knowledge ethicised and filtered behaviour within venues, often referred to by workers in terms of 'us and them' (Hochschild 1983). Because the customers' familiarity with their assumed roles, inside the café and bar spaces, was so unpredictable, workers were required to think and act on the spot—a defining element of *Toyota-ism* more broadly (Hardt 1999). Postmodern production allows room for unpredictability or flux in the productive model by dancing with the consumer rather than predicting their course of gratification, reinforcing the deeply collaborative nature of generating surplus value from what Gregg described as the *production cultures* (Gregg 2009; Hardt 1999). Indeed, workers faced an unpredictable patronage on a daily basis and were forced into temporally managing their relationships with the public based on the customers' behaviour and their degree of taken-for-granted knowledge. Although many standardised tasks were highly structured and even militant in their execution, it was the human aspect that required the workers' adaptability and flexibility in approaching each unpredictable encounter.

Reference list

Bell, D 2011, 'Hospitality is Society', *Hospitality and Society*, vol. 1, no. 2, pp. 137–149.

Carah, N 2014, 'Brand Value: How Affective Labour Helps Create Brands', *Consumption, Markets & Culture*, vol. 17, no. 4, pp. 346–366.

Felton, E 2012, 'Eat, Drink, and Be Civil: Sociability and the Café', *M/C Journal*, vol. 15, no. 2. Available from: http://journal.media-culture.org.au/index.php/mcjournal/article/view/463 [18 September 2015].

Foucault, M 1990, *The History of Sexuality Volume One: An Introduction*, trans. R Hurley, Vintage Books, New York.

Gill, R & Pratt, A 2008, 'In the Social Factory? Immaterial Labour, Precariousness and Cultural Work', *Theory, Culture & Society*, vol. 25, no. 7–8, pp. 1–30.

Gregg, M 2009, 'Learning to (Love) Labour: Production Cultures and The Affective Turn', *Communication and Critical/Cultural Studies*, vol. 6, no. 2, pp. 209–214.

Habermas, J 1991, *The Structural Transformation of the Public Sphere: An Inquiry into a Category of Bourgeois Culture*, trans. T Burger & F Lawrence, MIT Press, Cambridge.

Hardt, M 1999, 'Affective Labor', *boundary 2*, vol. 26, no. 2, pp. 89–100.

Hardt, M & Negri, A 2000, *Empire*, Harvard University Press, Cambridge.

Hardt, M & Negri, A 2009, *Commonwealth*, Belknap Press of Harvard University Press, Cambridge.

Hochschild, AR 1983, *The Managed Heart: Commercialization of Human Feeling*, University of California Press, Berkeley & Los Angeles.

Jameson, F 1998, *The Cultural Turn: Selected Writings on the Postmodern, 1983–1998*, Verso, London & New York.

Lazzarato, M 2006, 'Immaterial Labor', trans. P Colilli & E Emory in *Radical Thought in Italy: A Potential Politics*, eds. M Hardt & P Virno, University of Minnesota Press, Minneapolis, pp. 132–147.

Lobato, R 2006, 'Gentrification, Cultural Policy and Live Music in Melbourne', *Culture & Policy*, vol. 120, no. 1, pp. 63–75.

Massumi, B 2002, *Parables for the Virtual*, Duke University Press, Durham & London.

O'Connor, J 2004, 'A Special Kind of City Knowledge: Innovative Clusters, Tacit Knowledge, and the "Creative City"', *Media International Australia*, vol. 112, pp. 131–149.

Rocca, MD 2008, *Spinoza*, Routledge, New York.

Sennett, R 1998, *The Corrosion of Character: The Personal Consequences of Work in the New Capitalism*, WW Norton & Company, New York.

Snyder, B 2016, *The Disrupted Workplace: Time and the Moral Order of Flexible Capitalism*, Oxford University Press, New York.

Spinoza, B 1996, *The Ethics*, trans. E Curley, Penguin Group, London.

3 The customer is not always right

'Feel your crowd': the force of the first encounter

Unlike *emotional* and *affective labour*—as being performed by a burdened worker and consumed by a demanding customer—in the 'hip' economy of this research it is reaction and contagion of all engaged 'players' that determines the quality of the product (Hardt & Negri 2000; Hochschild 1983). Much of the job of 'affected labourers' is the gauging of customers: not only to watch them, but to probe and then await their response before saying and doing the next thing. "Picking your crowds" and "gauging patron's needs" were widely referenced skills and defining features of the job across the spread of interviews because, as Jack said, "everyone is different". Jack outwardly told me that people-watching—which happened a lot behind the bar—was also a significant aspect of postmodern society and web 2.0 culture, adding that the job had endowed him with many life skills useful for dating, namely learning how to read and relate to people, and building self-confidence. "It's all about the timing," he told me. "I hate that when you go up to someone and you're just off, it's so awkward!" (Jack). What Jack and others shed light on is that the initial force of encounter cannot be entirely scripted, but rather it must flow from the initial affect, and, more specifically, the worker's resultant gauging of the customer and appraisal of their reaction—much like everyday life encounters in general. Moreover, the importance of *both* the customer and worker being affected respectively reiterates the way affective value renders labour less about performing for the needy customer, and more about 'everyday' organic exchanges that rearrange the traditional commodity–money–commodity relation (Smith 2012).

Sam, a barista working in Northcote part-time while studying international relations, told me that the initial greeting with his customers both "set the mood" and (with a sarcastic tone) at the same time it did not go "much further than that initial thing". His seemingly contradictory thinking reveals the critical split-second force of encounter—between workers and their customers—as determining their relationship thereafter. Hence, if it doesn't go well, following Sam, it won't go "much further than that initial thing". I asked him to elaborate on why the initial encounter simultaneously "sets the mood" and, yet, doesn't "go much further", and he was hesitant to say that service was meaningful, and refrained from relating the service one receives with the creation of a memorable café experience (Sam). However, he did express the power of a positive first greeting, explaining hypothetically that if he was greeted by someone happy, it would be the first person he meets, which "sets the mood for your experience there, but I don't think it goes much further than that initial thing" (Sam). Sam was, as I have introduced him, cynical, as a result of the lack of respect he had been shown in his time working in cafés, and somewhat disenchanted by his exposure to public sociality at its apparent worst. But importantly, implicit in his dialogue is the strength of the initial affect, which echoes a range of conversations I had with other workers. At another café, which was an iconic Fitzroy worker's cottage converted into a café affected with a homely array of worn cookbooks, knitted teapot warmers, old wooden dresser tables, antique teaspoons, and the like, I had a coffee in the homely courtyard with Jane, who expressed, many times, the value of the initial affect. At one point she said, "I think with that first hello, their response to that is big as to how we go from there. You get people that instantly you just know, oh they are going be a pain, often from that initial greeting" (Jane).

I asked Jess what the impact of a hypothetical scenario would be if a customer, upon their initial interaction, smiled back at her, and she knowingly assured me of the impact of this mutual exchange in gauging "whether someone is going to be good to talk to, or good to engage with". She told me:

> Oh, yeah, it's like instantly, cause that's always a moment of terror, like, 'Hi . . . how are you?' Like, sometimes I cannot project as well as I should and then if they just ignore you, either because they didn't hear you or they are an asshole, that moment of terror . . . of like, 'Oh, God, give me something back!' But yeah, that's how I indicate whether someone is going to be good to talk to, or good to engage with.

Similarly, Aroha, a waitress at the café in Collingwood, while speaking on the topic of "annoying customers", lamented,

> There's some people that go into cafés and just want to make you feel shit. They feel an ego trip or something, and you can see people who are like that as soon as they do say 'hello' to you.

Aroha, Sam, Jane, and Jess all place value on the split-second judgement, and the passion it engenders, which is situated within an unpredictable context. Like the temporality of *Toyota-ism* in allowing markets to dance with consumers, rather than predicting consumer behaviour, thinking in 'the moment' is also a necessary requirement of workers, that is, gauging how to approach their customer as 'affected labourers' (Hardt 1999). Arthur, who worked in downtown Melbourne having moved from Norway, drew on his own experience as a fellow consumer hypothetically walking into a cocktail bar wearing a hoody. He explained that too often he had entered bars in a hoody and with what he considered to be a relaxed disposition, and the worker had said to him, in a pretentious tone, "Hello sir," which he saw as a lack of "feeling the crowd" (Arthur). He said: "I don't know if there is any specific technique, it's just about who you are as a person. It's like meeting a random person at a bar or at a gig; you just act the same way" (Arthur). Service styles rely on mutual smiles and initial judgments and feelings rather than performances, per se.

It actually seemed that across the venues, styles of service and *emotional labour* more generally were less of a priority than refining the systems for getting the product to the customer and perfecting the atmosphere, as a product, by solidifying its vibe (Hochschild 1983). The performances of service were just one part of the affective package, demonstrated in the stripping away of clichés and performances, which were replaced with a rawer style that was reflective of the reality workers faced—that is, the customer is not always right! The staff were emphatically clear to me about how little value service held for them—when they were the ones who were customers in Melbourne's cafés and bars. Sam, for example, continuing our discussion about rapport with customers as not "going much further than that initial thing", explained that he lived on Sydney Road in Brunswick, which is another gentrifying northern suburb housing many café and bar venues, and it wasn't good service that drew him back to any particular venue. Actually, he clarified, it was the overall 'quality of the product', and he said, "I'll just choose it on the day. There's nothing that'll, like the service won't draw me back there—it's more just the quality of the product. I usually don't dwell on the service" (Sam). The quality of service in 'hip' venues has remarkably limited relevance in light of the intensely affective and aesthetical vibes and products being sold that, in many ways, do the work for them. Sam did go on to reveal, however, that if he was in a better mood, he'd go a bit further, and Jess, too, said: "I think it's mood dependent, so if I'm in a good mood I'll go above and beyond. If I'm not having a great day, I'll try and just get through it." In fact, it was the fact that he was friends with the owners of the café before working there that had prompted him to give better service, illuminated in his comment: "Because they're my close friends and it's like—seeing their business do well, so that kind of element does kick in every now and then" (Sam). The affect that customers and venues have on workers determines the way they approach their job.

The more the patron adhered to *feeling rules*, the further out of their way the staff member would go to serve them (Hochschild 1983). Stacy explicitly said to me, "If they're regulars we are more likely to change how we do things for them," before adding that, because the café she works at does things differently to a lot of other specialty coffee shops, the staff do "put the pressure on them [patrons] to understand why we do things the way we do it". Their service was tied up in their efforts to help the patron relate to them and their venue, to help the customer understand the process and ideologies promoted in the given venue—to appreciate the job they were doing. Workers were signal points in this sense: curating the behaviour of the venue's patronage by making it transparent what was involved in the process of serving them. I sat in the café in South Melbourne one afternoon—the one that is off an inconspicuous laneway covered in graffiti.

The café promotes messages of sex, drugs, and rebellion through its coffee delivery vehicles parodied as drug courier vans, cult-like merchandizing and branding, a menu with semi-pornographic wordplay for food descriptions, a factory-like open-plan atmosphere, and a 'we don't care how loud the music and coffee grinders are' attitude. Without the workers' tattoos, modern haircuts, sense of style, or ear stretchers, for example, it simply would not be the same space—because the ethical and ideological messages would not be so clearly communicated. What transpired was an aligned logic between the venue's atmosphere and the workers' *habitus*—a term Pierre Bourdieu (1990) coined. *Habitus* refers to the systems of dispositions and exteriorisations that denote notions of class, and therefore differentiate groups through the ideological value and symbolism they carry with them (Bourdieu 1990). What is particularly useful about this concept is its emphasis on both the autonomous actions of individuals, *as well as* the influence of the social field they are located in, that together inform the individual's tastes, dispositions, and beliefs (Lloyd 2012). Following Lloyd (2012, p. 620), "habitus is an active component in the psychosocial processes that shape behaviour. These internalised dispositions fundamentally affect the way we 'read' a situation". The visual cues and workers' *habitus* sent affective messages into the spaces, as customers became aware of the feel of the place by what was given off by the embodiments of the people in it (Bourdieu 1990). In fact, I caught myself amused on a few fieldwork visits to the South Melbourne café, which, during the week, hosts mainly office workers wearing suits and often having business meetings. The workers' cultural embodiments could not be further from those of the 'suits', which was the term used by workers to refer to these customers, as they would stand side by side discussing coffee—but the workers appeared to always hold the upper hand in the interaction (Bourdieu 1990). I fancied that this was almost as if, unlike in ordinary everyday life, these mostly very young, low-status, low-paid workers were able to escape being socially beneath the 'suits': it was their venue and they knew it.

'Affected labour' is most clearly defined by the affect the productive process has on labourers themselves, and, in this sense, the generation of 'hip' immaterial value takes place on a multidimensional interactional pane that is a product of 'the moment'. This is expressed in the ubiquity of gauging work, which determines the workers' approach to service thereafter—as an 'affected labourer'. This reiterates that *both* the customer and worker need to be positively affected for the rapport to build and the service relationship be a success. Most workers' approaches to service were actually efforts to help the patron relate to them and their venue, and to help customers understand the process and ideologies promoted in the venue. Workers are vibrant signal points in this sense: curating the behaviour of the venue's patronage by making it clear what is involved in the processes of café and bar service, and whether, indeed, the customer is 'an asshole' (Jess).

'Hip' ecologies of interaction: transparency

Being moving and doing 'affected labour' is not defined by the militarisation of smiling and various versions of 'Hi, how are you?' uttered one hundred or so times a day in return for a wage. Nevertheless, it may be part of the working reality of service workers, which theories of *emotional labour* have captured through concepts like *deep* and *surface acting* (Hochschild 1983). But, looking through a feeling lens, rather than a strictly *emotional labour* lens, captures the breadth of sensory signifiers influencing workers themselves, and such feelings induced in workers and employers help determine product value; the customers' feelings are just one aspect of the affective package. Affects create sedimentations of past feelings, which are reactivated through collisions between bodies and objects, nostalgic sensations, atmospheres, and which many staff described as the 'vibe' (Massumi 2002). In the previous chapter, I described the saturated market of cafés and bars in Melbourne as having developed largely through these venues' commitments to harness, solidify, and replicate not just visual aesthetics associated with the products and spaces but, perhaps more importantly, the ethical and ideological messages that sit within the frame of the product's narrative. Venues clearly fetishised their particular atmosphere and product of service, which became a vehicle for instituting the venues' and workers' ethics, heavily reliant upon their customers having the sensory perception to appreciate, engage, and buy into the vibe of the place.

Overtly displaying items and relying upon "the quality of the product"— which Sam said determined his choice of café on Sydney Road—means venues can push the emerging new product as well as signify themselves as on-trend and upbeat in an ideological sense. Following Lazzarato (2006), affect produces the "cultural content of the commodity" which defines and fixes cultural standards and public opinion (Lazzarato 2006, p. 142). The products of *immaterial labour* are ideologically enlarged, and, as such, they generate surplus in a market saturated with multiplying arbitrary commodities all competing for distinction and differentiation. As the iconic dank café and bar in Fitzroy started to populate early one Friday early evening, mulled wine was being poured at the bar and a customer came up to order another drink by saying "Can I have a mulled wine, now I've seen it?"—the visual cue proving to be more efficient in cueing the customer as to what they could potentially order, than, say, looking through the menu to find a drink. In cafés, too, it was common to present all the new and less well-known coffee on full display, like the non-pressurised coffee, for example, which is a newer method of preparing coffee that uses a filter rather than the espresso method.

Because venues place such an emphasis on solidifying their vibe, the product, in turn, is more affective; less pressure and attention is on the worker to create the venue's message and perform for their customer, because the abundance of atmospheric affects do much of the service for workers. Renditions of service, then, are based on affects encountered by workers themselves more than the traditional cliché of 'service with a smile' or 'the customer is always right'. In fact, styles of service were dependent on a sort of mutual recognition between the customer and worker and, in exposing their labour efforts, workers regularly defended everyday laws of respect, commonality, and common sense. In this way, the transparency of workers' labour efforts functioned as a means of communicating to the customer what is actually involved in getting the product to the seat—especially when they were dealing with demanding or ignorant customers, who affected negatively and who were portrayed through an 'us and them' mentality. Seemingly simple movements, like stirring drinks on the bar ledge or pouring latte art, were a point of affect, reflected romantically in Jack's pointing out of instances where "they all go silent". But, perhaps more importantly, they were *explicitly revealing the labour time to the viewer.* Where so many services go to the greatest of lengths to hide and conceal their efforts in providing their product, hospitality embraces the visual display and craft of presenting food and beverages. In fact, Zara pointed out the potential sympathy and satisfaction from customers as long as they could see that the staff member was working hard, saying, "I think if you're honest with them, and if they see you're trying hard, they won't give you grief." Transparency aids the creation of the affective environment for the consumer to fit into, while helping workers navigate the obstacles imposed by serving the public.

After ordering my drink from Zippy one evening at the bar in Collingwood, which specialised in Cuban whisky and was decorated with imagery of iconic American baseball players and Che Guevara memorabilia, she explained as she made the drink just how much "love" she had put in because it required her to get the bottle of gin from the storage room that was up many flights of stairs. With a chuckle, she said, "The fruits of my labour right here!" Although Zippy's tone was parodic and perhaps even sarcastic, she nevertheless communicated her labour time to me and was completely transparent about the processes of the bar. On another occasion at another venue, as I stood in line to order my drink I overheard a customer who, having waited in the line for some time, said, "It's a lot of work, isn't it!" In other words, workers did not shy away from exposing their labour efforts, or from communicating to their customers what was actually involved in getting the product to the seat. They emphasised this when explaining that "normal people" fail to understand hospitality from an industry perspective and the taken-for-granted knowledge that the industry generates and relied upon, which they all portrayed as 'us and them' (Aroha; Zippy). A large portion of service actually involved educating and keeping customers up to speed with insider knowledge, as well as guarding against 'them'—the disrespectful and unfamiliar customers.

When the dishwasher at the café in South Melbourne came in and out of the barista's section to stack clean saucers, the internal division of labour was made especially transparent—the kitchenhand stood next to the barista, who was tattooed, had severely combed-back hair, and was dressed in contemporary swag, while the kitchenhand was an older man, visibly doused in sweat, and the only one wearing an apron. He seemed almost too terrified to look up. But aside from the exposed division of labour, what this kitchenhand's presence came to outwardly reinforce was that hospitality is hard work, and there is more to it than tends to be assumed. Also, the common practice of workers placing tea towels in their back pockets, or over their shoulders, is symbolic of the trade or craft— something for customers to see and to be reminded of. Similarly, the bartender's cocktail shaker represents an identifiable symbol and visual cue, as does the use of the old-fashioned kitchen bell. Despite the level of technological change to docket systems and the use of iPad till systems, the kitchen bell remains the, slightly parodic, symbol of slave status. And, as I sat at the bar down an inner-city laneway, during an uncomfortably busy evening, big bags of ice were being carried right through the middle of the packed bar during mid-service, with its silhouette hanging from the unfazed bartender's back. Across many venues, it felt like there were no real attempts to mask noise; in fact, often there would be a heavy bass in the sound system or metal on wood from all the tamping; at one of the venues there were tradesmen drilling and building next door. In Collingwood at the café, a classic 1990s hip-hop track came on and the barista raised his hands and began waving in relief as if to say 'thankfully this is on!' Several of the staff, like dominos, broke into rhythm, dancing to their specific tasks. Moreover, in both cafés and bars, things like gesturing from across the room, negotiating where to wait for a takeaway coffee, or getting the attention of a waiter, all functioned more effortlessly through physicality than one-way verbal communication, and while deliberate or not became affective and trans-parent visual aspects of the venue's atmosphere and its *feeling rules* (Hochschild 1983). This hospitality without hospitableness, or hipster Melbourne service, *is* the interactional ecology of *transparency*.

In fact, the manager of the café in North Melbourne called out to me as soon as I walked in one day, "We're about to hit lunch"—which workers often commu-nicated to customers to inform them of the system so that they would understand the process and, hopefully, exhibit more taken-for-granted industry knowledge and patience. I often overheard the workers explicating the venue's system to the customer. Rose, for example, asked the customer where they wanted to sit, and, when they did not know where, she was quick to point out, "Oh, it's just easier if we know where you are sitting so we can get the order sent there." To another customer who was waiting to pay their bill at the till, Rose began the dialogue by saying, "Let me put this coffee order in before it escapes me." So, in both instances, Rose could communicate to the customer through exposing exactly what was involved in serving her customers. In Northcote, I noticed espe-cially the degree of communication involved in the worker's relationship with their customer, like when Jess saw a customer eyeballing her from the till as she was arranging cakes in a cabinet. She called out to them, "Let me just package some cakes up for this girl and then I'll be right with you," rather than something more disguised like "I won't be a minute." Instead, she chose to explain to the waiting customer what exactly she was doing and why she could not serve them then and there. Furthermore, it was not uncommon for customers to wait at the till for a few minutes while such priorities were taken care of first, such as deliver-ing coffees without milk because they have a golden crema in the espresso which will dissolve fairly quickly and lose its effect; delivering Long Black coffee was prioritised over attending to the customer.

By making their labour efforts known to the customer, the pantomime dynamic felt increasingly parodic in tone, where the workers' production of service, and the laborious work involved in gauging unpredictability and reasoning with the affects, often slipped into an exaggerated display that was prided, uninhibited, and hence imitative or pantomime-like. As I have explained, traditional notions of hosting and being hosted are either devalued and dismissed, or constantly blurred, crossing over seamlessly between worker and patron (Bell 2011). On countless occasions, I saw trivial conversations take place between staff and patrons, which would become satirical to watch and very playful as staff would float in and out of passionate banter while completing their many tasks surrounded by an expectant crowd of waiting drinkers. I watched one customer, for example, tell the barman during a busy period that his friend had fallen off his bike on the weekend, while many patrons waited in line to be served by the barman who was engaged in seemingly frivolous conversation with this customer. Moreover, the workers' twenty- or thirty-minute breaks, in almost all venues, were spent inside the establishment, often out the front among customers eating. The times I would visit one of the cafés tended to coincide with the manager's break—he would sit next to me on the 'leaner' (the bar ledge that separates the front from the back of the café and bar spaces), hurriedly feeding himself and working on the café's weekly roster on his laptop. And at the other end of the spectrum, at the café and bar in Fitzroy, I watched a customer stand and wait at the bar while Stacy, the bubbly manager, called out to all the staff that they were having tequila shots together, and said, "Who wants one?"

Workers made assessments of their customers, commenting to one another, and at times took on overt bodily displays including laughter and shocked facial expressions. Sam even explained the ridiculing involved in dealing with "shit customers" just to "get a smile out of it". Giggling, he proudly told me:

> We all work together so if we know someone's going to be a shit customer, or something, I think there's quite a few, we just kind of make a joke about it the whole time. So every time we're going to go to their table we'll just be waiting for their reaction. Yeah, be nice at the time and then come back and we'll all just kind of pay out on them. [Laughing] Shit, not the nicest thing, but we'll get a smile out of it!

By parodying the "shit customers", workers found common ideas with one another based on their exposure to undesirable feelings induced by "customers at their worst" (Sam; Zippy). On another evening at the bar in downtown Melbourne, a cosy, eccentric, tiny little space off one of the city's famous laneways, and, from what I was told, one of the oldest cocktail bars in the city, along with the Fitzroy venue I mentioned earlier, I observed parody as a clear technique in the bartender's logic of transparency. A somewhat rambunctious customer was ordering, but in hindsight she was more demanding than I initially perceived. She seemed drunk. Here, the bar was busy, and I felt the bartender grow agitated. Instead of getting angry or putting up obvious boundaries, the bartender 'killed' her drunk customer with a parodic display of kindness. In a well-enunciated, strong voice, the bartender projected her chest forward and gave the customer direct eye contact, nodding as she assured the customer, "I'll just charge you now, my love," stretching her arm forward to gesture for the customer's cash. She pushed the receipt into the customer's hand, saying, "There you go, my darling, I'll bring it over to you, thank you darling girl" (Evie). This was much like Sam's statement that "sometimes I'll be overly nice to people I just wouldn't usually be nice to"— the killing-with-kindness mentality and quick slip into parody pursued by Evie and others. Parody, therefore, was part of the broader repertoire of techniques of 'affected labourers' for coping with the affects and their unpredictability or the 'them' of their venue's patronage.

Even clothing becomes a medium for parody, self-satisfaction, and ultimately detachment. I spoke to one bartender at the Cuban-themed Collingwood Whisky bar about the bright top he was wearing during the shift, which was a kitsch 1990s-style Hawaiian shirt with images of garish cocktail glasses printed all over it. On another visit, I realised he was wearing a very similar one, only this week it had big images of bananas instead of cocktail glasses on it. He said proudly to me, "It's a bit weird on the tram and shit, but once I'm here it's fine" (George). I asked him whether he wore them solely for work and he said he used to, but not anymore. "I am married, I don't care," he said. "Even if people are laughing at me or think I'm weird, it still makes them happy" (George). In other words, he found ways to deal with, and overcome, the foibles of his patrons' conduct. In many ways, parody aided this process of detaching from the unpredictable customer, in preference to a more playful, looser mindset, like George's approach to what he wore to work. This satirical and playful approach to the demands of customers, and the potential mundanity of the shift, also enabled a degree of control over the customer. I watched one evening as three female customers gazed at the bartender as he made their cocktails, before taking their money, grinning with a real glimmer in his eye, knowing that at any point he could deny the infinite thirst of the drunk, which he acknowledged later in our conversation: "At any time I can tell them to leave" (Jack).

Affected service is less about performance and the customer's feelings, and more about the affect the productive process has on labourers who are 'users' of the venues, too. This is expressed in the interactional ecology of transparency that was deployed by workers, to aid in their dealing with the "asshole" customers and their unpredictably *negative* effect on workers (Jess; Zippy). By using parody and pastiche and revealing their labour time overtly to the customer, in order to deal with affective encounters of a negative kind, workers enforce the ethical codes of the venue, exposing the level at which the customer was required to fit in to the venue.

Fit in, or fuck off

In producing the atmosphere of the venue, workers represent 'us' through their distinction from 'them'. They communicated this by being transparent about the work they were doing, which, in turn, forces customers to fit in to the vibe of the venue and encourages many *customers to positively touch workers*. Their *habitus* sends signal points curating the behaviour of the space (Bourdieu 1990). In many ways, being known and recognised at people's regular landmark provided workers and patrons alike with an anchor in their subjective exteriorisation, while helping workers guard against and detach from the unfamiliar or disrespectful customers. One afternoon at the café, as a customer walked in the door, Rose immediately called out from behind the coffee machine "I haven't seen you today," before the customer went on to lovingly explain that it had been his first week at university. Rose then remembered, piecing together the recollection that he was at the café when he had just received his high school results—both parties appeared chuffed at their shared memory of this moment. In other words, their relationship helped solidify their respective identities in their search for the common part of their, seemingly, very different lives.

The aesthetical coherency of workers as engaged 'players' in the creation of a vibe, which helps to articulate the venues' aesthetical and ethical messages, are common in 'hip' Melbourne cafés and bars. I would often watch people sitting up at the bar engaged in conversation with the bartenders, or the bartender being referred to as a "superstar" by a customer, or a group of young men sipping coffee over the bar as they yarned together with the barman about growing different types of beards, clapping and laughing vivaciously. As well as highlighting the product's overall affect—as workers represent and communicate the ideologies of the space—their camaraderie also forces the customers to fit in to the vibes of the venues. Customers are required to fit in to the venue after being seduced by it, reflected in the 'us versus them' mentality expressed by so many workers toward those they are serving. As such, they placed a strong *emphasis on the whole* which transformed into the mentality that it is better for everyone to be happy than appeasing specific individual demands. As Jack put it, "The thing we have to take into account is trying to control people's behaviour to make it more pleasant for all of the customers in the bar." The individual customer is not necessarily the first priority; rather, the holistic system is—workers do not appear to feel the need to pander over their customer, nor treat them as their master in the traditional sense of service: the customer is *not* always right.

Paradoxically, within the venues where workers did not smother their customers in their presentation of service, it appeared that the customer was more inclined to express the pleasurable affect it had on them. In fact, often customers would display a sense of pride in paying, or would engage in a volleyball-like game of gratification and affective contagion. One evening, for example, as two customers walked out of the tiny cocktail bar filled with lanterns and warm lighting, I watched from over my shoulder as they walked toward the door raising their arms flamboyantly at the barman who had served them their drinks, even shaking the bartender's hand before parading a final salute from the door as they left. I asked Rene, the now quietly esteemed bartender, if he had met the customers before; he had not. This was not the first time I saw this proletarian paradox play out, whereby the customer or the master of the scenario sought to impress or gratify the staff member, having been moved with a sense of luck to have been at the venue, prompting their overt demonstrations of gratification.

The erosion of traditional oppositions like master and slave, or front stage and back stage, coupled with the transparency of the work involved in providing the particular affective world, create a pantomime of both mastery and subservience where customer and worker float in and out of each other's roles and which manifest in the venue's ethics of service (Bell 2011). Moreover, this interactional ecology supports Hardt and Negri's (2009, p. 303) conviction that "an individual can never produce the common, no more than an individual can generate a new idea without relying on the foundation of common ideas and intellectual communication with others". At the three-storey bar in the old building downtown, it was a quiet early evening service—I was one of only a few sewing-machine tables—and a group of customers arrived and sat down on the low armchairs before requesting the bar's music be turned down. Barney, in an assured tone, explained to them, "We cannot turn down the music any more without losing the atmosphere of the bar." Sometime afterwards, as Barney and I chatted from opposite sides of the bar, a screeching laugh erupted from the table. Barney, in the same blunt tone and wearing a melancholic expression, said to me, "See, if I did turn the music down, that laugh would have cut through the entire bar." As well as determining the demands of the customer through a holistic common-sense outlook, I was struck by how frequently staff would ask "Have you been here before?" as their way of judging the person's degree of familiarity with them and their venue and its particular style and system.

Customers were encouraged to fit in to the venue, rather than expecting the venue to meet the needs of every customer, as in the 'customer is always right' maxim, and it is in this sense that the 'hip' economy functions in excess to the material commodities it enlarges. The value of the immaterial commodity lay not solely in its affected consumer, but also in the ideally moved creator of the product. As well as affect being a tool of labour that the workers expected to use, or at least hoped for their patrons to affect back to them, the workers wanted to be affected, too. Zippy revealed this as we sat outside on Smith Street:

> It's all give and take, it's all about the customers. I think if the general public knew how they could affect the people who are serving them, that would really change the way I think people would behave. Because if you have a good night, even if it's busy or quiet, a good night is where you have nice people come in who are polite and easy to please, and just generally nice. A bad night is when you get assholes in basically who have, you know, no sort of regard for you whatever, anything: your venue, or your space, or your job, or how hard you're working or whatever. It all comes down to the interactions you have with people. Because, you know, it doesn't matter if we're busy or not, we could be slammed, but if everyone we're serving is really nice then I'm more than happy, it's a really good feeling. All it takes is a please and thank you. It's really simple.

If the customer doesn't not invoke interaction, if they don't engage, then it is unlikely that the staff member will. At the bar in Fitzroy, with its countercultural rebellious feel, it seemed that the more the customer played up to their vibe, the more joyful the staff became. And if they did not play up to anything then the staff treated them in the same way, which appeared from the outset as the cli-chéd inhospitable snobbery of hipster Melbourne hospitality service. Passion and affect were contagious, intensified by the unpredictable patronage and their lack of taken-for-granted knowledge that I outlined in the previous chapter.

But when customers displayed something identifiable to the staff, something attached to *their* nature, dynamics changed and attempts at rapport became visible. Thus, workers didn't rely on the praise derived from satisfied customers, but when they were positively affected, for example, by receiving a smile or some other form of appreciation, they appeared to be affected powerfully. Jasper explained this reality of good service as requiring "a bit of give and take on the other end", because, while he is trying to make the customer as comfortable as possible, he isn't trying to make them happy if they already aren't when they come in. Across the range of interviews, an overwhelming range of staff expressed the importance of not taking things personally and how one must remember that although there are difficult characters, not everyone is "like that" (Jasper). So, detaching to varying extents and accepting people's individual quirks were paramount to just getting through, if not doing well in the job.

Many lived near their places of work, which created networks around the venues. The hidden landscape can be navigated through (but not limited to) the inner northern suburbs that are densely populated with 'hip' hospitality venues. Industry networks helped to 'set to the scene' for customers to (ideally) fit into. This was illuminated to me as I watched a group of baristas discuss 'coffee roast profiling' and 'non-pressurised espresso' techniques, one afternoon, at the Collingwood café. One of them had finished his shift, but stayed to chat with the group of customers who sounded like they, too, were part of the industry. And, across venues, friends of the staff would be crowded around the leaner or the bar, talking with bartenders, almost creating the core atmospheric hub for other patrons in the café to see and follow—so that they, too, could better understand and fit in to the vibe of the venue. In the bars, especially, it felt like friends and industry insiders were relied upon to set the scene and get the party started, so to speak. Angus, for example, told me that "there's probably about six or seven bars where all the bartenders know each other and go to each other's work". Their collectively established their 'us' mentality, which was reflected in the networks and relationships formed autonomously among colleagues and across the industry. In bars, particularly, this largely came down to the culture of finishing the shift and having a discounted drink at the venue, which was common across all the venues. As Stacy pointed out,

> We all hang out but, like, I think if we all hang out we hang out here, or at one of our other venues, you know? I guess you can drink cheaper here, pretty much everyone who knocks off sits around.

And across the venues it was clear that during the shift, while working, staff were developing a rapport and relationships with one another in and around the work being done. Jasper explained, "During the day we're socialising all the time, so while we are here it's kind of a very social time." However, interestingly,

Jasper did point out that as a manager he tries not to blur the two, because the more they are mixed, the harder it becomes to manage: "Because you need to kind of go: 'I had a really lovely time on Saturday and, oh, there's a guy on table 71, you need to go see him.'" Although morale was extremely high, this was not necessarily reflective of life outside work and the venue. In other words, the vivid sociality happening within each venue and across industry networks is contained within these affective worlds. As Stacy put it, "I guess hospitality is a little bit incestuous like that." This further reinforces the notion that the affect venues have on workers is just as important as the affect they have on customers.

Informal cheerful chats over a drink during the night's downtime, or quiet periods with few customers, provided self-governed moments for staff, regulars and, more commonly, hospitality workers from nearby bars and cafés, to all congregate and be customers. Furthermore, during such moments, *hostguesting* reappeared in that staff found themselves occupying the position of their dialectical counterpart: benefiter of the hospitable space (Bell 2011). Venues almost functioned as if they are the workers' home for friends to do the rounds of visiting their industry mates, as traceable sources of their identities, an observation which many workers explicitly shared with me. Jess, for example, expressly likened pulling one's weight in the café to doing the dishes for her "shitty flatmate". I saw many people come into the venues who seemed to know the workers as more than simply customers. In fact, Zippy told me of one particular phenomena whereby "there's this sort of trend happening at the moment where a lot of well-known bartenders are just sort of doing their rounds around the city, doing rock star shifts"—where bartenders do a one-off shift at another high-profile bar.

The networks of bars and cafés within the inner northern suburbs anchored both staff and patrons in their subjective exteriorisation, while enabling both to buy in to the culture of the particular venue. Stacy pointed out, "We get a lot of coffee geeks in and that's great; they are a huge part of our coffee side of business." Jane, from the café that was a converted house in Fitzroy, linked the "nice customers" that she gets at the café with all the likeminded hospitality staff working in the area of Fitzroy, attributing this to why she felt the café had "a lot of really nice customers . . . because they go to work at night and then they're on the receiving end, so they know." As 'affected labourers', workers used *transparency* to curate the patronage by encouraging customers to fit in to the vibe of the venue. This is why the patronage of venues so often reflected its ideologies, aesthetics, and affects, and was reinforced by the networks built around the industry. Crucially, such networks tended to stay inside the venues, seducing workers in their generation of profit perhaps just as much as they affect their customers who are *not* always right. Like 'users' or consumers, if workers are moved by production, they will likely affect (others).

Summary

'Hip' commercial atmospheres provide an opening or invitation for the customer to identify with the ideologies being communicated through the venues' emphasis on vibe. This helps to communicate the product's cultural references, through its seductive atmosphere, so that less pressure and attention is on the 'affected labourer' to create the product's message and wow the customer. This was exposed in workers' approaches to service—gauging the customer with a uniform greeting, and then using the feeling produced by the encounter with the customer to determine their service thereafter. It was the customer's response that temporally informed the worker as to how much common sense and taken-for-granted knowledge they possessed, so as to gauge their degree of fitting in to the venue and its vibe. The interactional ecology of transparency hinged upon workers being invested 'players' just as much as customers: their degree of care was based on the customers' observance of the *feeling rules* of the venues and their amount of taken-for-granted knowledge of the industry (Hochschild 1983). Renditions of service, then, were based on affects encountered by workers themselves, illuminated in the workers' transparent approach. Moreover, workers needed to be seduced by the aesthetical and ethical atmospheres of the venues—exposed in the industry-wide networks built around 'hip' venues in Melbourne that, more importantly, remained *contained within the spaces*. The situational nature of industry networks and bonds reinforces the idea that it is the labourers, too, who are affected by the venues in a process that ultimately generates profit for employers, that is, if the worker trusts and represents the ideological enlargement of the venue. That the workers' degree of appreciation and respect toward the venue, and the lifestyle, determines their communication of the brand reveals the potential for appropriation by capital.

Reference list

Bell, D 2011, 'Hospitality is Society', *Hospitality and Society*, vol. 1, no. 2, pp. 137–149.

Bourdieu, P 1990, *The Logic of Practice*, trans. R Nice, Stanford University Press, Redwood City.

Hardt, M 1999, 'Affective Labor', *boundary 2*, vol. 26, no. 2, pp. 89–100.

Hardt, M & Negri, A 2000, *Empire*, Harvard University Press, Cambridge.

Hardt, M & Negri, A 2009, *Commonwealth*, Belknap Press of Harvard University Press, Cambridge.

Hochschild, AR 1983, *The Managed Heart: Commercialization of Human Feeling*, University of California Press, Berkeley & Los Angeles.

Lazzarato, M 2006, 'Immaterial Labor', trans. P Colilli & E Emory in *Radical Thought in Italy: A Potential Politics*, eds. M Hardt & P Virno, University of Minnesota Press, Minneapolis, pp. 132–147.

Lloyd, A 2012, 'Working to Live, Not Living to Work: Work, Leisure and Youth Identity Among Call Centre Workers in North East England', *Current Sociology*, vol. 60, no. 5, pp. 619–635.

Massumi, B 2002, *Parables for the Virtual*, Duke University Press, Durham & London.

Smith, A 2012, 'On Shopworking', *New Left Review*, vol. 78, no. 1, pp. 99–113.

4 Behind bars

A logic of detachment

View from the top: the social platform in affective workspaces

The intensity of 'hip' café and bar atmospheres, and their affective communication of an image, does much of the job for the service worker in wowing their customers, meaning that less pressure and attention is on them to create the product's message in the traditional sense of 'service with a smile'. This is most obvious in the interactional ecology of transparency that I described in the previous chapter, where they let the sensory stimuli of the brand do much of the performance for them, while they made it abundantly clear to the customer what is actually involved in serving them. This inversion of the commodity–money–commodity transaction that is present in traditional theories of service work—where emotional and *affective labour* are conceptualised as being created by an employer and performed by an exhausted worker for a demanding customer—reveals that in 'hip' economies the value of service is not so one-dimensional (Eden 2012; Smith 2012). The sensory intensity circulating within the spaces meant workers were immediately presented with an image to embody, and thus a visceral social platform to distinguish 'us' from 'them'. Inside these spaces, workers became aesthetic signal points curating the behaviour of the venues' patronage and, in doing so, they embodied the venues' aesthetical and ethical messages. So, the mental platform of the venues aided workers' confidence to detach from the negative feelings induced by 'outsiders' and the effort involved in providing traditional five-star renditions of 'service with a smile'. The enlargement of the venues' vibes, ethics, and atmospheres was emotionally contagious, not only for customers to react to and embody, but workers were touched by it as well. The mental elevation felt by 'affected labourers' put them in a position where they could detach from the seriousness of service and assert their ideas about the 'nature' of things (Virtanen 2004).

The mental 'platform' felt by workers, because of the sensory stimuli of the venue as an assemblage with its own coordinated identity, was produced in part by the organisation of the physical spaces and the dynamics they engendered. For example, the actual position of the bar, or counter, which separates the workers from their customers, physically elevates them to a position of authority, distinct from their patrons, and ultimately provides them with the confidence to observe and assess the public they are serving. In fact, during my beer with Jack, at the bar in Collingwood when I had ignorantly asked for a whisky sour, he placed his arm on the bar ledge behind him and began patting it, and, grinning from ear-to-ear, pointed out how useful the physical barrier of the bar was in controlling his relationship with patrons—telling me, "That's why this thing is so good." Throughout our conversation, Jack constantly pointed out how the bar functioned as a physical barrier, a way of stepping back, holding the encounter at arm's length and maintaining a mask so that "when you're on the other side of it, it's very different". In cafés the position of the coffee machine seemed to function almost like a 'spotlight' monument, representing a common symbol of knowledge and culture and imparting a sense of confidence and safety for workers as they hovered over it. Symbolic objects, like the coffee machine, help to protect workers' identities just as much as they communicate the identity and prestige of the space to the customer.

Workers frequently observed, reflected, and commented on their clientele from the 'platform', which appeared to them an authentic source of knowledge that was grounded in reality. As Arthur said: "It definitely makes a difference. You notice a lot more when you work behind a bar, you observe more." In fact, many found pleasure and joy in the 'people-watching' aspect of their work. Jane, for example, told me she did not want to continue working in cafés but could not see a way out, knowing that her preferred vocation was knitting and that it would provide little chance of employment. However, expressing pleasure in the sentiments that the job did provide her with, she explained that it was the people-watching element and "the little things" that appealed to her—"what they're doing, and who they're with, and what they're talking about together, and where they've been, and where they're going, and that kind of stuff" (Jane). I watched two waitresses stand and whisper to one another from behind the counter, every now and again glancing up at certain members of their audience, and I realised that more generally, workers were actively distinguishing themselves from their audience at work. This collegial relationship, through their collectively established identity within the venue, or 'us' mentality, was something they bonded over as 'affected labourers' (Clough et al. 2007). A vivid memory comes to mind here from a night's observation work at the little cocktail bar in the inner city. It was packed, but I had managed to grab one of the three bar stools, while patrons hovered behind me, bantered, and ordered their drinks over my shoulder. I sat scribbling in my notebook while constantly being tapped on the shoulder and forced to explain to tipsy patrons why I was, supposedly, writing in my diary in the middle of a raving bar. Sitting squashed next to me was a female patron, probably in her forties. She was with her partner and visibly intoxicated, propped up at the bar as she hopelessly swayed on her stool and muttered indecipherable words to the bartenders. As the two patrons, themselves, appeared to realise they were unfit for another drink and left, the bartenders proceeded to discuss them: who they were, what they were about, what they had been doing, and why he was not drunk. Workers' exposure to the social body, such as the previous scenario, reflects the many opposing ideas they are confronted with, which initiate their commentary and observation on the social 'platform' of the venue.

Workers' affirmations and observations with one another around common ideas, in what Virno (2004, p. 49) describes as "the life of the mind", reiterates the significance of the feeling that the production process had on workers. I explained in the previous chapter that, because of the centrality of observing and gauging people, the job gives workers a certain freedom of mind to develop an understanding of the endless demands—and thus colours—of the social world around them. Moreover, their 'gauging' and social commentary, as well as the constant forces of encounters they faced, meant that the job pushed them to develop an understanding of 'nature'. Akseli Virtanen (2004) cites Marx (1993) in his description of the *affective labourer* as defined by his or her understanding of 'nature'. Virtanen (2004, p. 223) suggests, *affective labour* is "neither direct human labour the worker performs (shaping materials of nature, producing new objects, etc.) nor the time he or she expends". Rather, pace Marx (1993), it is:

> The appropriation of his own general productive power, his understanding of nature and his mastery over it by virtue of his presence as a social body—it is, in a word, the development of the social individual which appears as the great foundation-stone of production and of wealth.
>
> (Virtanen 2004, p. 223)

Here the author distinguishes *affective labour* by its enabling of the individual worker to generate their own affirmation of the 'nature' of things through their very exposure to the social body. Virtanen's (2004) *affective labourer*, then, has an education in experiencing the colours of the social body and the public spaces where individual bodies and ideas collide, at a café or bar, a doctor's office, a classroom, or on Instagram, for example. The social body, in other words, is the coming together of individuals and objects passing on affects to other bodies, which may not collide ordinarily (Williams 2007).

Indeed, on the social platform of the venue, staff seemed to express greater confidence in asserting their commentary and observations and, ultimately, in alignment with Marx (1993), Spinoza (1996) and Virtanen (2004), they were able to affirm the 'nature' of things. For example, when I spoke with Aroha over a pint at a nearby pub in Collingwood after her shift at the café, she explained the process of "rising above" and being the bigger person as an ultimately liberating experience. This, she said, was a matter of hospitality workers needing to swallow their pride, but she quickly qualified that this could be done

> in a way that doesn't make you feel like you are belittling yourself like, you can actually hold it, and I think sometimes it actually makes me feel stronger that I know I can rise above these asses that try to make it hard for me, or think it's fun to come into a café and do that.

Not only is Aroha's comment indicative of her detachment from "asses that try to make it hard", in that she can "hold it" and "swallow her pride", but she also illuminates the experiential material that she could access in finding virtue in such negative affects, which she describes as ultimately making her "feel stronger". Many workers developed, over years of working in the industry, deep experiential archives that they readily accessed in confronting and reasoning with the many negative affects they encountered.

The 'affected labourer' is required to make sense of their subjection to opposing ideas, minds, and bodies through their own experiences of being affected. And, like Zippy and many others point out, the workers' exposure to public sociality, often at its worst, presents them with a platform from which to interpret everyday life and draw from their past experiences with the social body. Feelings happen when individual bodies collide with other bodies and objects—and their opposing ideas—which thereafter become engrained experiences that create much of the individual's "epistemological fabric of ideas", and from which they can draw in subsequent affective encounters (Deleuze 1988, pp. 74–75; Seigworth & Gregg 2010, p. 3). Being around opposing ideas, that is, by being 'affected labourers', initiates workers' observation and the expression of their ideas from the mental 'platform' that they are on inside their place of work. As Caroline Williams explains, commonality can only be the result of the coming together of individuals—in effect, "common notions thus find their conditions of *possibility* in the resources of the collective imagination, and their mode of *expression* within reason" (2007, p. 363, emphasis in original). Further, their experience of being affected led many of them to detach and escape private introversion so that they could, drawing from Jasper, "observe, assess, and work out the best outcome for the business".

The correlation between service workers and 'social individuals' is further illustrated in the emphasis workers placed on *experience* as paramount in being a good bartender or barista (Virtanen 2004, p. 223). Jasper put this in terms of avoiding micromanaging the workers in the café, because they needed to grow into their role through the harshness of experience: "All people needed to grow into their job and without letting them know, I'll always be there to fix it." Zippy also told me that while the more arbitrary and baseline tasks can certainly be taught (like placing orders on the electronic till or memorising the liquor selection), other more social and interactional, or even intuitive skills, simply cannot. In both Jasper's approach to encouraging his staff to fix things themselves and Zippy's opinion that interactional skills cannot be taught, the worker is expected to draw from their own personal archive of experience to deal with the unpredictably human nature of the job. Zippy went on to say vehemently that one cannot learn how to make a drink unless they're making a drink for a customer: "You can learn all you want about what glassware to use and this and that and how to use a double strainer, but there are certain skills you can't teach, like personable skills." Knowledge of the ways of the patronage, from the workers' perspectives, was portrayed as a certain way of seeing things. Although Zippy went on to describe the negative long-term repercussions of her bartending job, namely the demands of working nights and sleeping during the day and the repercussions on her general health, what resonated with her significantly more strongly was the way the job taught her "to be tough". She said, "I think it teaches you to be tough. At the same time it definitely teaches you how to deal with people." Arthur, too, said the barman's ability to conduct meaningless conversation with strangers "definitely makes a difference; you notice a lot more when you work behind a bar, you observe more".

While most workers did not think that the skills required in their job were determined by their individual character traits, inasmuch as many of them saw themselves as unsociable in their private lives, or 'nerdy' and 'geeky', most participants *did* overtly emphasise to me the resilience required in hospitality work, which, many pointed out, simply cannot be done by everyone. Jasper was honest about the harshness of the work, inasmuch as it was inevitable in hospitality that eventually "someone or something will destroy you". Or, following Spinoza's (1996) formulation, they will be affected with forms of sadness, anger, and resentment—the negative affects—which are more difficult to reason with internally compared to positive and pleasurable affects that confirm the person's ideas, and thus tend to be more easily understood. Jasper, for example, believed:

> As soon as you get into hospitality, you're going to get kicked in the ass by a bunch of people and you're going to feel like crap. Someone's going to come and destroy you and go, 'Oh, whatever,' and walk out and you quickly learn that that's not such a great thing, and I totally understand why a lot of people go, 'Nah, not for me.' Like, a lot of people just go, 'I could never do that.'

Stacy, too, illuminated that on several occasions her partner told her that he could never do what she did, which she identified as a common and reasonable perspective toward hospitality work. In other words, negative affects, which are an inevitable outcome of service work, generally, bewildered those who had not experienced hospitality work. For workers with deep experiential archives of negative affects to draw from, such negative encounters provide potential to detach through pastiche, parody, or exposing their labour efforts to the customer with transparency.

Venues put workers on a platform where they were freer than they ordinarily would be to assert their social commentary and order the negative affects that are ubiquitous with their jobs. As well as the spatiality of cafés and bars, which provided them with a social platform at work, it was the venue's affective atmosphere, projected through its vibe, which workers represented, curated the patronage with, and used to detach from their serious self, by dissolving into the ideological enlargement of the product. Like Carah (2013, p. 364) describes, "affective labour is fundamental to a mode of branding that creates value by stimulating and modulating a general circulation of meaning within a communicative enclosure". It is the affective space—the venue's image and brand—that creates the *communicative enclosures* which workers embody, develop, extend, and communicate as 'affected labourers' (Carah 2013, p. 364). Venues provide workers with an atmosphere and identity—a social platform where they engage in social commentary supported by their confidence to affirm the 'nature' of things (Virtanen 2004). And, in this sense, they affirm a sense of reality about the 'nature' of things, in accordance with Virtanen's (2004, p. 223) discussion of the "social individual". The 'social individual' or 'affected labourer' is further reiterated by the experiential emphasis workers place on the job as something that cannot always be taught in the conventional sense (Virtanen 2004, p. 223).

'Hip' ecologies of interaction: detachment

During my conversation with Jasper at the café in Collingwood, he told me about the extent to which customers have complained about their experience there. Regarding one particular online complaint, he said that there had been a comment picking out one particular staff member. This confounded Jasper, who wanted to say that:

> You don't have to choose to come in here. You can go, 'I really didn't like it,' and then go somewhere else. But to come to a place and then, yeah, not have a great time and then go onto the internet anonymously and pick her out as someone, I just look at that and go, 'Why would you do that?' Like, I don't go into an office and go, 'That guy with the brown hair in the red jacket, he was really horrible.' I go into many offices and go, 'I can understand why this is happening,' but no one comes into a café and goes, 'Oh, I can see maybe why she's not having a great day.'

Jasper reveals a common lack of reflexivity in approaching the worker *as a person*—instead, the reviewer treated her as a target, as if she were a willing participant in some sort of contest. Similarly, Zippy expressed how counterintuitive the job was to the "normal reality of things. You don't go to any other place and demand something, and then complain that it wasn't exactly what you wanted. It's very weird, it's very interesting." The vacant behaviour of customers, or 'outsiders', where they did not display enough (taken-for-granted) knowledge, was commonly observed among such workers as Zippy. In fact, I often overheard customers almost threatening the staff with how much time they had before they had to leave. Aroha even pointed out several customers in the cafés who she found particularly rude, telling me that she had served many older women who felt threatened by her in front of their husbands. Such customers had even told her, "I don't want you to serve," to which she'd laugh and simply say, "OK."

When I met Zara at the end of the day where she worked as the host at the South Melbourne café, as she drank wine out of a mug through a straw while the other workers cleaned up the café for the day, she accentuated the constant effort made, which is not uncommon in low-status work, to uphold and, if need be, defend her affected self and precarious status through that instantaneous first encounter. She told me that she felt as though she was always trying to qualify who she was at the café, by the nature of her being in front of people all the time. She elaborated, as she grew visibly stressed by the idea of her being so misunderstood in the public eye: "People come and they assume, like, it happens everywhere, especially in hospitality, though it's a very heightened version—it's all about appearances, first impressions, and in that you're dealing with one-on-one service, one person's experience." Indeed, most workers expressed a strong desire for the customer to 'get it' in the face of daily demands from the possibly naïve stranger which, as I explored in the previous chapter, produces the 'us' and 'them' mentality possessed by so many workers in their gauging of their patronage. But the customers' misunderstandings of the person behind the role is commonplace and worth little serious rumination from the perspectives of the workers.

It was the negative feelings induced by patrons' lack of taken-for-granted knowledge, and their treatment of workers more broadly, that mobilised their *detached interaction*. Stacy, for example, was acutely aware of the detached role she knew she presented to customers, as she told me what she found hardest about her job:

> Dealing with people that think you're a dickhead when you're not. You're just doing your job and you've got to put on the mean face and say no, and some people can just be really awful about it when they're really drunk.

The most difficult aspect of Stacy's job as bar manager, she felt, was her feeling misrepresented when customers thought she was "a dickhead", because she was forced into "dealing with people" who do not relate to the role she is forced into embodying, simply by doing her job and putting on "the mean face". But she was able to reason with the feeling induced by drunk customers and disengage accordingly. Being misrepresented became the hardest part of her experience as an 'affected labourer', which she detached from by qualifying: "but I know it's a job". Zippy also explained this insightfully, as we spoke while the early evening downtime allowed her a moment to talk. She had a higher education degree in architecture, travelled extensively, and had a lot of experiential wisdom to draw from in discussing interactional labour in the bar. When I asked her how much she felt her interactions at work affected her, she explained the irrelevance of the worker's dignity during encounters at work because "you really see all of humanity, all colours":

> You can't take people seriously, and there's a running joke amongst hospitality workers—the fact that the longer you work in hospitality the more you grow to hate people, and, it's not true, like it's not the truth, but it's a good way of sort of describing the experience. Because, you see people at their best and at their worst, you really do, like—especially on a Friday or Saturday night when it's busy and they're drunk and everyone wants to drink—you really see all of humanity, all colours.

The growing to "hate people" of which Zippy speaks, while she qualified that "hate" may be too strong a word, was nevertheless a common experience born out of seeing the customer "at their worst", the customer's ignorance of the systems and the job, and their dismissal of the staff member serving them. Thus, as she put it, "you can't take it personally".

For Spinoza (1996), inability to moderate and detach from affects defines the notion of *bondage* and, conversely, the more the individual moderates and reasons with the affects, the more independent their ideas are likely to be, and the more liberated they will feel, which he describes in terms of *adequate ideas*. That is, the mind's understanding and knowledge of the *cause*, derived from prior experience of having dealt with similar feelings (Williams 2007). He explains that affects are adequately reasoned with when the individual grasps the cause rationally, by placing it in line with the other ideas that constitute the person's mind—what Deleuze (1988, pp. 74–75) describes in terms of the mind being an "epistemological fabric" comprised of pre-individual ideas (Spinoza 1996). By optimising one's *adequate ideas*, the person seemingly has accumulated an ever-greater repertoire of experience to draw from and reason with (Deleuze 1988). For an idea to constitute adequacy then it must be placed "within the series of ideas currently constituting mind" (Brown & Stenner 2001, p. 93). That is, adequate thinking happens when one reasons with, and reflects on, past experiences of similar affects—what Deleuze (1988, pp. 74–75) describes as "the epistemological material through which the idea refers to other ideas". *Adequate ideas* are the result of the affected person's knowledge of the cause; the result of their prior experience with similar affective intensities, or, the scope of their experiential archive (Deleuze 1988; Spinoza 1996; Williams 2007).

It is the presence of oppositional ideas to one's own that help to shape the person's sense of self, and the 'adequacy' of their ideas (Spinoza 1996). This is important because the more one is exposed to opposing ideas, the more affects one will have experienced and hence the more common notions the person will have accumulated (Massumi 2015). In this way, following Carnera (2012, p. 78), in order for adequate ideas to formulate "we need to experiment with our own experience". Sharp (2007, p. 745) says that a person's *adequate ideas* gain force, not necessarily because they are "the truest ideas, but the ideas with the most life support, as it were, from fellow ideas". Identifying common notions amidst the chaos of affect enables one's *adequate ideas* to evolve as one tries to understand affects according to the commonality between things, rather than according to the irrational passions "connected with the idea of external things" (Williams 2007, p. 364). This is why Spinoza (1996) suggests that the 'adequacy' of most ideas emerges out of affects loosely attached to joy and pleasure; because passions associated with sadness, including hate or anger, tended to restrain the body, rendering the affected person more likely to inadequately and irrationally understand the cause. Put differently, it is harder to reason and digest pain than pleasure. In this way, the formation of *adequate ideas* "is a question therefore of whether we have the strength and the power to question our own values. Do we have the strength [potentia] to do this [*sic*] fully knowing that it involves a level of pain?" (Carnera 2012, p. 81, brackets in original).

As we sat in the café courtyard at the end of her shift in Fitzroy, Jane told me about a customer that she served on the weekend who ordered a meal that came with hummus, and the customer had sent it back because the hummus had supposedly expired. But Jane knew for a fact that the hummus was homemade the day before and so, swallowing her pride, and ecological sensibilities, she threw it away—"I don't like food wastage but we had to throw it out and make it again without the hummus for her, so yeah, but you know it's not major I don't think, but little things". Apart from the frustration of colliding with these sorts of café characters, Jane made it explicit that it was not major, but insignificant in the broader context. Zippy also pointed to this in alluding to the degree of subservience and detachment required to stay in the industry or get good at the job. She used an example of a typical 'idiot' customer coming in to the venue and giving her crap from over the bar. In this case, she explained, she couldn't step up and demand an apology. Rather, she said,

> It's no skin off [her] back. They can do what they want as long as I'm giving them a good time and they walk away feeling they've got their money's worth, then fine, it doesn't affect me, it shouldn't change the way I am, it shouldn't devalue the way I see myself.

But Zippy saying that she was not especially bothered by annoying customers does not render her unaffected; rather, detachment is a reiteration of her being an 'affected labourer' (Spinoza 1996). Zippy's ordering of the feeling motored her detachment, whereby she drew from her mind's experiential archive to reason with negative affect. Like Spinoza (1996) explains, detaching from negative affect is part of the ontology of being affected. In fact, Zippy's conviction that "as long as I'm giving them a good time and they walk away feeling they've got their money's worth, then fine, it doesn't affect me" suggests the priority, and even the source of satisfaction, as fulfilling the customers' basic needs, period. Zippy's perspective that although customers have the potential to be disrespectful this should not necessarily diminish one's 'dignity' at work echoed other workers' comments, reiterating their detached approach.

Most workers that I spoke with had been in the industry for a number of years, telling me that their experience had directly shaped many of their ideas associated with being affected, particularly those of a negative kind, further reinforcing the experiential description workers gave of the job. Jacob, for example, explained that "the longer it goes on, especially after sixteen years, I play up, but I don't let it affect me and the decisions I make". Sam also told me that, by working in the industry, one is able to see the triviality of many issues and is consequently able to let things go more easily, such as forgetting a customer's food order. Stacy also highlighted the importance of gauging the customer, before explaining the importance of not necessarily reasoning with a drunk customer. This meant she could guard her sympathetic and vulnerable side in order to get through the job. She told me that she had learned to be firm and "a little bit tough" depending on what the situation was. For example, if she was dealing with a "boozy" customer she would have to say no to them right from the get go. The more reasoning that she gave, or the more that she sided with them, so to speak, the harder it was to detach, because all she wanted was for them to understand her more. But, as she said, "It's harder, sometimes, to be like 'No, not today,' and just leave it and be straight faced," because if she expressed that her "sympathetic side" was vulnerable she was more likely to be pushed by her customers: "I would love to be like, 'I can't, man—you know how it is, I don't want to get into trouble,' but then I don't want that kind of sympathetic side to come out and then people can push you."

For Jane, if the customer was invoking negative affect or if she was personally "having a shitty day", it would be up to the customer to engage her and, if they didn't, she didn't see it as her responsibility to go out of her way to wow the customers through her service. Through exposure to the affects in all their chaos and unpredictability, 'affected labourers' develop strategies to deal with the unpredictable range of people, most visibly through their detached and transparent reactions (explored in the previous chapter). The workers' level of engagement was largely determined by their affected experience, where their degree of care was based on the context of how they are feeling at the time and the initial force of the encounter. Indeed, workers are affected by the production process, as reflected in the interactional ecology of detachment, whereby, experiencing the many negative affects implicit in frontline work more generally, they detached from and restrained the unpleasant feeling seemingly in accordance with Spinoza's (1996) formulation of *adequate ideas*. In this way, the logic of being affected *is* detaching from painful or *negative affect*.

Pastiche, misrepresentations, and smokescreens

Venues—as intensely atmospheric, ideological, and seductive spaces—elevated workers into a position where they were free to detach from the negative impact of rude or unforgiving customers, and become "social individuals" (Virtanen 2004, p. 223). They detached from the negative affects they encounter to guard themselves against with the unpredictability of the public—which produces the hipster service that is, ironically, ubiquitous with Melbourne's affective café culture. If, however, the customer was to positively influence the worker during their initial interaction, then the bond and rapport developed between them and service became more five-star, so to speak. Illuminatingly, because it was the venue, rather than the job, that put them on a social 'platform', their confidence and elevated position was *situational*, and, as such, often misrepresented the workers' identification with their serious and private selves. One of the first myths debunked in the field was my assumption that it must be extraverted characters drifting into these kinds of jobs, based on their intrinsically social and performative propensities. In fact, I would often sit in the venues and think to myself, 'Surely introverts would find this job difficult!' On the one hand, there were workers who felt like they were naturally suited to the work, often describing the pleasure at seeing a satisfied customer, or by being a 'people's person', or natural socialiser. For example, Zara said, "You have a sense of control of the whole place when you're doing it right, and I'm naturally good at that and I love doing it, and I love making people feel excited, and happy, and looked after." Olivia, too, when I asked her what other work she wanted to do in the future, said, "It will always be really people-based and interaction-based. I could never really do anything behind the scenes."

On the other hand, I was inundated with staff telling me that, contrary to what their work roles might paint of them, personally they were not very outgoing people, outside of work. Sam said, for example, "Usually outside of work I'm a very quiet guy, and just like, not outgoing in that sense at all, so it is putting on that persona." Jess, too, thought she wasn't very outgoing outside of work, in the sense that she would never go up to a random person and say hello unless she was prompted to do so: "It's very funny because in that setting people like us are put in that awkward thing of like—I've never seen you before but I have to say 'Hi' first". The café puts her on a platform, compared with other parts of her everyday life—such as if she goes to a party—where she is not as socially elevated as she is at work, but when she's "behind the machine and someone walks into the café you have to learn in that setting it comes naturally now, but in other settings—no way!" Similarly, Zippy said the bartenders she works with are "awkward" and "geeky" people who paradoxically "shine" behind the bar. It is the venues as affectively charged spaces that put workers on a social platform, which, in turn, provides them with the confidence to detach. As she said:

> If you don't have chat, then you're done. It's interesting because I think most bartenders are awkward people, like day-to-day. Like socially, if you see these guys outside of the bar in normal clothes, doing normal things, they're awkward, I'm awkward, we're all very, very, awkward people, and I think that's why we do so well in bars is because we might be awkward day-to-day but behind the bar that awkwardness is a strength. Everybody's very nerdy, very geeky—you're talking about guys who know the citric properties between oranges and lemons. It's where awkward people come to shine.

By pointing out the degree to which venues elevated workers who ordinarily would be "awkward", Zippy's comment reveals the way in which being affected by the venue empowers her to assert and affirm her ideas (Spinoza 1996; Virtanen 2004).

Zara, as I relayed, had said she was naturally good at making people feel excited and, what's more, loved doing it, while at the same time explaining that she was insecure and self-conscious in her private life, despite her coming off as confident. The irony that an industry predicated on affects, senses, and sociality is represented by mostly "awkward people" speaks to the broader pastiche embedded in consumer culture in postmodernity (Zippy). In an important text, *The Cultural Turn: Selected Writings on the Postmodern, 1983–1998*, Fredric Jameson (1998) tells us that pastiche parallels the notion of blank irony in postmodernity by its *imitation* of the *uniqueness* in original traditions and styles. The author distinguishes between parody and pastiche, both of which help define the postmodern cultural logic. Jameson argues that, while parody and pastiche both serve to mimic original forms, pastiche is a neutral form of parody in that its mimicry is ambiguous and seemingly unintentional:

> Pastiche is, like parody, the imitation of a peculiar or unique style, the wearing of a stylistic mask, speech in a dead language: but it is a neutral practice of such mimicry, without parody's ulterior motive, without the satirical impulse, without laughter, without that still latent feeling that there exists something normal compared to which what is being imitated is rather comic.
>
> (1998, p. 5)

Mirroring statements made by Zippy, and many others, the author expresses the vagueness of distinguishing between peculiarity and normality in examples of pastiche. Indeed, this pastiche smokescreen—wherein staff were moving in and out of seriousness and frivolity, sympathetic to the original form of hospitality and craftsmanship, yet at the same time ridiculing and exaggerating aspects of it—added to their repertoire of techniques for coping with the affects (Jameson 1998). Furthermore, the social 'platform' provided by venues enabled the workers' use of pastiche, freeing them to dissolve their serious self into the ideological and affective enlargement of the venue (Lazzarato 2006).

Most workers knew they came across as pretentious or even dismissive, which was reinforced through the mental elevation that they embodied inside the venue, because they had detached from negative affect, using pastiche to ridicule the encounter with the intention of lessening its force, without the customer realising it had ever even happened. Angus spoke about the contradiction between the workers' representations, and particularly the stereotype of bartenders as "pretentious", compared with their individual character, private self, and projected identity outside of the venue. In doing so, Angus reveals the "blank irony" or pastiche in the network of bartenders he knew (Jameson 1998, p. 5). Talking thoughtfully, as we sat upstairs in the adjoining bar, bright red satin and velvet covering the entire floor, walls, and ceiling, and tasselled lampshades hanging very low, he said:

> It takes itself very seriously. But then I could think of many ways in which that's not true. But, I think that's something that would only be evident if you knew them, 'cause like if you didn't know these people personally and you walk into the bar and they've got a waistcoat on and a luxe moustache and they're playing with dry ice, then like the first thing you're going to think is, "Oh yeah that's kind of like the cliché," you know, pretentious cocktail scene, but knowing the person you can see that's it like they do—they are actually doing it and you can't argue with that, but you can also see that it's not really that serious.

The clichéd "pretentiousness" of Melbourne's bar industry, of which Angus spoke, actually masked the workers' (perhaps) more common experiences of awkwardness in the interactional ecology of detachment. That is, by moderating and detaching from negative shocks through their various approaches to their hyper-real service, workers (albeit often unconsciously) formulated coping techniques.

The venues, as affective spaces, empower the workers in them to observe, assess, and critique their patronage by providing them with a set of ideologies to embody, rather than their confidence being born out of a deep calling or the practice per se. In this sense, the actual 'hip' spaces put workers in an elevated position—or on a platform—to assert their opinion or 'come out of their shell', so to speak. But, because their being boosted is created from the affective enlargement of the venue, the platform misrepresented the individual workers, who were actually often using pastiche, parody, and detachment by exaggerating and blurring the line between seriousness and playfulness (Jameson 1998). Feelings are superfluous to the material commodity and capitalist transaction, inasmuch as they exist according to their own ecologies, rather than according to the ethics of capitalism or the commodity–money–commodity transaction, or the principle of private property (Tsianos & Papadopoulos 2006).

Summary

The collectively established 'us' that workers portrayed was supported by the mental platform on which venues moved workers, and, in turn, this enabled their "affirming nature" and their becoming the "social individual" of which Virtanen (2004, p. 223) speaks. This is further reflected by the industrywide connections and networks but, while common networks and camaraderie were evident inside the venues and during the shifts, workers emphasised that the sociality happening within the venues tended to stay inside the venues. The atmospheric workplace provided workers with a 'platform' where they could engage in social commentary at work, and these social elements of the job were emphasised, too, by the experiential emphasis through which workers described the job—as something that couldn't be conventionally taught. Indeed, staff spoke about the strength and resilience required as being much more crucial than possessing some 'natural' ability with people, performing, and/or sociality, and this, they pointed out, was a job that simply couldn't be done by everyone. Because of service workers' exposure to affects and their chaotic and unpredictable quality, much of the job was their being forced into reasoning with the causes and common notions attached to the countless negative collisions and encounters, which they most commonly achieved through detachment (Spinoza 1996). Experience had taught them to detach from the unpleasant feelings induced by "annoying customers" through using pastiche to ridicule their service (Aroha). In fact, most of the time workers detached until the customer affected them positively, in a process of affective contagion; the workers wanted to be affected, too. Their interactional ecology of detachment was often an outcome of their feeling misunderstood as they portrayed the stereotype of snobby inhospitable hospitality, further underscoring the 'us and them' mentality. Although the platform workers felt, and were affected by, inside the venues they worked freed them from the significance of service and trivialised the job in order to cope with the barrage of negative affects they constantly faced, it was precisely because their elevation was enabled by the space and the venue that their mental elevation was rendered a *situational* representation of the individual worker and their identifiable sense of self outside of work and the venue.

Reference list

Brown, SD & Stenner, P 2001, 'Being Affected: Spinoza and the Psychology of Emotion', *International Journal of Group Tensions*, vol. 30, no. 1, pp. 81–104.

Carah, N 2013, 'Brand Value: How Affective Labour Helps Create Brands', *Consumption, Markets & Culture*, vol. 17, no. 4, pp. 346–366.

Carnera, A 2012, 'The Affective Turn: The Ambivalence of Biopolitics Within Modern Labour and Management', *Culture and Organization*, vol. 18, no. 1, pp. 69–84.

Clough, PT, Goldberg, G, Schiff, R, Weeks, A & Wilse, C 2007, 'Notes Towards a Theory of Affect-Itself', *Ephemera: Theory & Politics in Organization*, vol. 7, no. 1, pp. 60–77.

Deleuze, G 1988, *Spinoza: Practical Philosophy*, trans. R Hurley, City Lights, San Francisco.

Eden, D 2012, *Autonomy: Capitalism, Class and Politics*, Ashgate, Burlington.

Jameson, F 1998, *The Cultural Turn: Selected Writings on the Postmodern, 1983–1998*, Verso, London & New York.

Lazzarato, M 2006, 'Immaterial Labor', trans. P Colilli & E Emory in *Radical Thought in Italy: A Potential Politics*, eds. M Hardt & P Virno, University of Minnesota Press, Minneapolis, pp. 132–147.

Marx, K 1993, *Grundrisse: Foundation of the Critique of Political Economy*, trans. M Nicolaus, Penguin Group, London.

Massumi, B 2015, *The Politics of Affect*, Polity, Cambridge, Oxford & Boston.

Seigworth, GJ & Gregg, M (eds.) 2010, 'An Inventory of Shimmers', *The Affect Theory Reader*, Duke University Press, Durham & London, pp. 1–25.

Sharp, H 2007, 'The Force of Ideas in Spinoza', *Political Theory*, vol. 35, no. 6, pp. 732–755.

Smith, A 2012, 'On Shopworking', *New Left Review*, vol. 78, no. 1, pp. 99–113.

Spinoza, B 1996, *The Ethics*, trans. E Curley, Penguin Group, London.

Tsianos, V & Papadopoulos, D 2006, 'Precarity: A Savage Journey to the Heart of Embodied Capitalism', *Transversal Journal*. Available from: http://eipcp.net/transversal/1106/tsianospapadopoulos/en [29 July 2014].

Virno, P 2004, *The Grammar of the Multitude: For an Analysis of Contemporary Forms of Life*, MIT Press, Cambridge & London.

Virtanen, A 2004, 'General Economy: The Entrance of the Multitude into Production', *Ephemera: Theory & Politics in Organization*, no. 4, vol. 3, pp. 209–232.

Williams, C 2007, 'Thinking the Political in the Wake of Spinoza: Power, Affect and Imagination in the Ethics', *Contemporary Political Theory*, vol. 6, no. 3, pp. 349–369.

5   Only give up on a good day

The force of pleasure in 'the moment'

Short-term trajectories

'Affected labourers' face a troubling tension: between enjoying the immediate benefits awarded by the job, and feeling stuck and unfulfilled in terms of their career and lifestyle desires, because the short-term benefits attach to the job largely make up for, or mask, its limited long-term vocational trajectory. Angus gave an insightful description of the pressure he thought all bar staff would ultimately face, inasmuch as if one was to move into a more professional hospitality role—like working for drinks companies, managing their own bar, going into consulting, or marketing and branding—they may experience forward progress in the industry, but they would still "seem to lose out on a lot of the other social elements". The immediate short-term benefits of having flexible hours, having a social job, and not being hugely responsible in the sense that there aren't genuinely important responsibilities entrusted in workers are attractive benefits that, for Angus,

> definitely have a tension with the feeling that you're kind of stuck in what seems to be an industry of short-term benefits and kind of low pay, where the forward progress isn't obvious and, when the forward progress is there, [it] may not be attractive.

In other words, the seductive qualities and immediate gratification awarded by the job were largely associated with its distinctly social nature, which Angus felt hospitality workers would lose out on if they were to move into more professional roles. Short-term pleasures obviate workers' desires for their futures, which are potentially unattractive, compared with the relative freedom allowed by the "social elements" of bartending (Angus). Indeed, research into what Rosalind Gill and Andy Pratt (2008, p. 15) call the *creative industries* finds that a "vocabulary of love" is a common feature of the affective workers' narrative, based on the requirement of a deep attachment and affective bindings to their place of work—and to the customers of their creative services—that are reinforced by the allowances these sorts of jobs make for the worker to self-express and self-actualise.

While detaching from undesirable feelings was an everyday, staple feature of the work—often ridiculing, parodying, or using pastiche to *adequately* order the unpleasant feelings implicit in their jobs as service workers—they were much less able to do so when confronted with *positive encounters* that had *outcomes accessible in the present*. As Spinoza (1996) explains, present and pleasurable feelings are the most physically intense, because they ultimately hold the strongest grip on the individual through governing much of their behaviour after that initial joyful feeling in the body takes place. Even though affects about future or past projections may be stronger, and more intensely felt, than those in the present, they nevertheless *directly impact* on the person's state in the *present moment* much more powerfully, and thus are more influential (Massumi 2015). Many workers joyfully described how meaningful and energising it was when customers positively affected them. Aroha told me that all of her "good customers" regularly tell her that they love what she does, and that was why she was there every day, or every second day. Positive feedback—from the customers that she approved of—was enough for her wake up in the morning when she didn't want to wake up, and "go 'ok', and when I walk in—it's on. It doesn't matter how hectic it is, you just get through it. There are so many different sideshows happening in the place". Aroha was "charged up", if you like, by all of those "good customers" who told her they loved what she is doing. Olivia, too, described the way encouraging reinforcement from customers pushed her "to keep doing it that way", and during another conversation with Aroha she thought, "When you excite other people, it's exciting." Jane, too, felt one affirmative encounter could empower her to do the same for others.

Sam found the fact that nothing was hanging over him, such as university work, particularly attractive: "When you get home and you're like, 'Oh, I could be doing this or this,' but, sort of, when the day ends there's nothing more you can really do except maybe be a bit better the next day." The transience of café and bar work—in that it didn't directly interfere with their lives after the working day ended—for Sam, and many others, was a desirable short-term quality of the job. Similarly, Arthur called out to me from over the bar one evening: "I enjoy the freedom and, to be honest, I enjoy the hours." For Stacy, it was the social nature of the work that affected her, so much so that she revealed: "I'd like to run my own business and have my vintage costume shop one day, but at the same time it kind of worries me how bored I might get, like, sitting in an office all day." During the same conversation, she also pointed out that her feelings were suited to the job because it is fast-paced; the unconventional shift work hours suited her, and she could likely find a job anywhere in the world. And Jess, who had a teaching degree but did not respect the education institution and so returned to hospitality, revealed that the stimulation and challenge of hospitality work was crucial in fulfilling her first priority, which was happiness. Her father had occasionally told her to "just toughen up" and "put [her] head down and get through it", but she couldn't understand this outlook on work, saying, "Maybe it's just a Generation Y thing, like, no, I don't want to do anything that's hard and unenjoyable, but I don't understand why you have to be unhappy, it just doesn't make sense to me." Hospitality work allowed her the stimulation to have the life she wanted, while enabling her happiness, which she contrasted with the unnecessary traditionalist industrial values of "working hard" and "toughening up" reflected in her father's perspective.

Jasper, too, described the encouraging touch of certain regular customers, as he recalled a group of office workers from around the corner that had relocated offices to Richmond: "So they're not here anymore, and that's kind of, like, a really strange thing and that really kind of affects us." The intimate relationships that workers organically developed with *certain* customers impacted them, and their decisions, much more than all of the 'idiot customers'. Jane, too, expressed how nice it was to have positive feedback from her regular customers at the café, when she told me, "It's just really nice to have positive feedback when you're at work and you get that here cause the food's good and the coffee's good." Indeed, workers often alluded, in a "vocabulary of love", to how joyful affects outweighed the many more negative feelings induced by some outsiders, from which they seemed to effortlessly detach (Gill & Pratt 2008, p. 15).

Workers were hesitant to project themselves into the future through their occupation, evidenced in the fact that most of them wanted to get out of the industry eventually. Angus said, "There is this tension, where it seems like an industry where there's maybe not an obvious way for forward progression or professional development." Joyful interactions in the present, rather than those which are projected into the future or focused on the past that tend to follow a more predictable script, are the most intense and influential in terms of the individual worker's capacity to act on feeling (Spinoza 1996). Indeed, many workers expressed a feeling of being stuck in the industry, and, as such, felt that it was extremely difficult to leave. Angus, for example, told me explicitly that "when you're in the hospitality industry, especially when you're young, it seems something hard to kind of get out of". Rob also explained the "slippery slope" involved in investing in the lifestyle of the job, which entailed a timeframe different to that of the mainstream 'nine-to-five' labour force:

> I'm looking at how to get out of hospitality at the moment to get some more practical experience in my field [robotics]. But I think I'll always be involved in hospitality to some degree because it is fun; if you find a good place, it is—it's a great time, and they essentially pay you to have a party every night. It's a slippery, slippery, slope I think, and once you're in it's kind of hard to find the time or motivation, mainly time on your days off, because it's pretty hard work—late hours and busy nights and usually working on weekends and stuff, so you might have a Monday/Tuesday off, and they're usually spent recovering, and then you're straight back into it. You don't really have time to find additional work.

Jane even told me that she would have to ban herself in the future from hospitality jobs because of the desirable short-term benefits it awarded her, even though she did not necessarily want to be in the industry and would rather be knitting for a living. She explained that it fits into the week wherever she wants it to, and even if she did have another job that occupied three or four days of her week she could still do weekends: "I can always fit it in somewhere, so yeah, I can definitely see it being hard to get out of." Jane continued to assert that, as well as benefiting from the lifestyle, she was also drawn back to the industry because she had experienced a fairly good run of previous employers, saying: "I could go back if I wanted to, so again that just makes it easier: I don't have to hand out resumes, I just have to make a call and ask for the shifts I want." Not only does she acknowledge the ease of accessing employment in the industry as influencing her career trajectory in general, she illuminatingly reflects on her personal investment in the venues that she has worked for, which provided her with a convenient network to find work, while benefiting her employer with a loyal employee.

'Hip' ecologies of interaction: ephemerality

There was an underlying contradiction implicit in almost everyone's narratives: while most workers gave highly descriptive and passionate accounts of their affectionate sentiments and attachments toward the venues in which they worked, illuminated in comments like, "I could talk about it all day," at the end of each interview, when I asked what their plans were, almost everyone said they didn't want to work in hospitality for too much longer. At the end of our conversation at the bar, over the road from the Northcote venue, Jess shook her head and said, "I enjoy it but it's not a future endeavour, that's for sure." And Jane, at the end of our interview, said, "I do eventually want to move into a different field. I'm not the typical people person, which I think you really have to be in 'hospo' [hospi-tality]". Zippy, too, despite embellishing her story of life behind the bar, told me at the end of our conversation: "I don't really see myself continuing to do what I'm doing, working behind bars and stuff. I think working behind bars has taught me a lot." Although the bulk of workers' encounters with patrons during their shift were somewhat muted, where they had learned to detach, ridicule, or even pastiche the interaction based on their experience and rationale of dealing with difficult customers, the strength of spontaneous joy resonated with them signifi-cantly more. While pleasurable transient encounters occurred less frequently, they were qualitatively more meaningful (than negative affects).

Their oscillation between loving and begrudging the job on a day-to-day basis illuminates the way pleasure in the heat of 'the moment' had a greater intensity and vocational influence than the (perhaps) more common painful collisions from which they detached. Johnny told me confidently that he had been in the industry for eight to ten years, and that it was when customers showed an interest, asked questions, or bantered with him while making their drinks that he felt fulfilled on some level; for him, this was enough to humanise a decade-long career that was never meant to be a career in the first place. Sam exposed this tension when he described the way the force of positive affects neutralised streams of nega-tive feeling. He explained that if he was encountering stresses at home, or had a 'shit customer' that meant he couldn't regroup, and he would think to himself, "I'm not going to be doing this forever," or "I've really got to get out of this. Come the next day I'll have a really nice day and I'm like, 'Oh, this is alright. I could do this for a while longer.'" When I spoke with Jane about what got her through the hard days, she said it was the hope of just one positive interaction that would outweigh all the other undesirable encounters she so often experienced:

> I just think that a really positive customer interaction can change your day, just one even. I used to work in the city at a really corporate café and half of the customers were horrible people—well, they weren't probably horrible people but they were awful to us, they weren't engaging at all, just be like, "Latte," and I'm like, "OK!" But what would get me through those days was the hope that one of those good customers would come in, and it totally changed my mood when they did, and I'd just be like, 'Right, OK,' just be happy about it, not grumpy. It just reminds me that you can be brought down by other people's negativity but if you're positive you can bring them up with your positivity.

Of all the "awful" people that Jane encountered and detached from, she remained hopeful that just one positive customer interaction would empower her to "bring them up" with her positivity. Rather than being affected in a literal sense, heavily burdened by a barrage of unpleasant encounters with rude and disrespectful patrons, being affected *is* detaching from negative or painful affects and embracing positive and temporal ones (Spinoza 1996).

That most participants found themselves still in the industry, despite their desire not to be, coupled with their affectionate description of the venue and job, defined by the seduction of a range of hard-hitting pleasures, indicates the intensity and force of joy in the short-term in precarious 'hip' economies. Like the fragility of living in 'the moment' in precarious life, affects are by nature fleeting, ephemeral intensities that capture the "this-ness" of everyday life; their intensification concerns an intensification of 'the moment' (Seigworth & Gregg 2010, p. 3). The job of workers in this research was predicated on ephemerality: the situational nature of the social platform that they were put on *inside the venue*; their transient embodiment of the collective identity of the venue; their relinquishing seriousness and projecting an ephemeral image; situationally-determined service styles or gauging work; spontaneous commentary from the platform which they may not necessarily have carried outside of the venue and off the platform; the flexible shift work hours; and the short-term job responsibilities. These transitory pleasures and advantages were more affective, more intensely felt, compared to the ways that negative encounters influenced them, and the way it impacted on their future projections—like their vocational trajectory and limited professional development or scope for developing their practice, or that they, in fact, didn't want to work with people at all. Indeed, workers wanted to be moved just like paying customers did; hence it was largely up to the customer to initiate commonality with the worker and venue, or instigate the interaction, before workers went any further than detached and satisfactory service, expressed in their logics of transparency and detachment. The power of the present moment in being touched by atmospheres and interaction was further illuminated by the overwhelming number of workers who told me how hard it was to "get out of" the industry, in light of the desirable short-term benefits it awarded them (Angus).

'Affected labour' is not only about the reactionary impact that products evoke in customers but, just as importantly, the impact the job has on the worker. Acknowledging that 'affected labourers'—and potentially *immaterial labourers* more broadly, although research has yet to be conducted here—are 'users', in both theoretical and practical everyday life discussions of contemporary work, takes us a step closer to "tarrying with time" and embracing the "margin of manoeuvrability" that defines affect and its potential to empower the body (Massumi 2015, p. 19; Tsianos & Papadopoulos 2006, p. 5). Massumi (2015, p. 153) sees contemporary consumption as a step beyond *niche* marketing and into a newer phase of *relational* marketing, wherein consumer choice tends to be affective rather than relationship-based, functioning through affective contagion to induct the individual into their ideologically "assigned role". Rather than addressing consumers as free agents, who make informed choices based on rational thinking, contemporary markets capitalise on the temporality of affect as a persuasive point of the consumers' *and* workers' propensities (Massumi 2015). In this sense, postmodern production recognises and manipulates the affective capacities of workers *and* consumers through accumulating surplus out of the rhythms of culture and the "entire time of life" (Hardt & Negri 2004, pp. 111–112).

Affected investments: identifying with the workplace

The interactional ecology of ephemerality is further shaped through the personal investment workers tended to make in the venue, lifestyle, and short-term rewards, in response to their being moved by situational joy. By investing, they sacrificed or made a kind of down payment through working longer, less regular, and more unusual hours, compared to the mainstream nine-to-five labour force. This rendered them tired of social interaction, and lacking motivation in their private lives. Yet it was these flexible shift work hours, etc., that were at the same time desirable benefits, which positively influenced them. Hence, they *invested*: they surrendered their long-term visions for the future and their lifestyles for the ultimately more seductive short-term pleasures. Jane, like many others, had found a venue to work in with which she could personally identify, which directly influenced her level of personal investment in the venue. She explained that because of the different standards and expectations of service across the industry compared with the venue she worked in, which did not have any formal service standards per se, she felt especially drawn to it. Her work, she felt, was especially relaxed in that she could get to know people and be herself, which was "a bit kooky, because there were no standards of service in the sense of 'Good evening, how are you this evening, have you had a wonderful day?'" Rather, she explained, "It's just like, 'G'day, what are ya doing?'" Adding to her sense of relaxed authenticity in the venue where she worked was her manager—Rose—who Jane felt that they were "lucky to have", thus illuminating how the workers' personal investment *was often about the venue and not necessarily the job.*

Although the lifestyle attached to the job was actively resisted by some workers, most participants embraced the personal investment or buy-in involved in enjoying the short-term pleasures derived from the job. Arthur, for example, put the personal investment made by workers in terms of their knowing deep down the quality of what they were serving and therefore essentially endorsing the venue, product, ethic, aesthetic, and so on. He said, "You could be very good in hospitality but be selling a shitty product, and then you won't be happy yourself because you know what it is." Rob, too, emphasised the relationship between positive affects at work and the degree of personal identification he had with the venue and, resultantly, the job at hand. He told me:

> It depends on the venue; not even the venue—it depends on your superiors. If you don't get that sense of worth out of your superiors then you don't contribute as much. The last bar I was at, I didn't have that sense of worth so I was like, "Eh, just sort of let things slide, don't worry about it," whereas when I was bartending in London, I loved the bar, loved the guys, everything like that, so it was like, "Every day pull your weight, do everything right, don't take shortcuts."

If Rob respected his superiors and the venue more generally, his work ethic would be stronger; he would very likely invest in the job and its accompanying lifestyle, as opposed to those venues where he does not "have that sense of worth". Similarly, Jess expressed her appreciation of the industry culture that revolves around specialty coffee like knowing the other baristas and waiters/waitresses and going out for breakfast to places where she knows the people working there. Appreciating, respecting, and personally identifying with the venue's culture determined the workers' level of personal investment in their workplace. Moreover, by developing seemingly authentic, organic, and loyal ties through their interactional labour, workers found virtue and greater meaning in the 'hip' work that they didn't necessarily want to be doing.

In one of the cocktail bars downtown, Jacob, now in the bar industry for ten years, described his entry into it as an accident. He explained that while many people worked in hospitality simply to "pay the bills" or support their study, for full-time staff there was a growing sense that the longer one worked in the industry the more "you sort of feel like you need to give a little back". In other words, the more experience workers had with being affected by working in the industry full-time, the more likely they were to—themselves—be affective or, in Jacob's words, "to give a little back". 'Affected labourers' are lucrative assets for employers, inasmuch as, by virtue of being affected by positive and short-term affects, they are more likely to act, to affect, personally invest in the business and, ultimately, be better workers. While Lloyd (2012, p. 631) states "it is no longer necessary to retain any sense of loyalty or identification with an employer because the labour market has shifted towards short-term, flexible, insecure contracts", this research reveals that workers are affected by the venue and this actually leads them to develop loyal networks and personal investments. That the venues and lifestyle appear to seduce workers back into the industry, despite their (often) idealised long-term vocational trajectories that can leave them feeling stuck, indicates their personal investment in both the venue and lifestyle attached to the industry. Like many pointed out, they work longer, non-standard, and on-call hours and, as such, often found themselves tired of social interaction in their private lives outside work. This was conflicting, because the flexible hours of work provide desirable benefits according to some workers. And this is precisely why they personally *invested*: they sacrificed long-term goals for the affectively, or ontologically, superior force of short-term benefits (Spinoza 1996). Zippy, for example, like many other workers, told me that she forced herself to "do normal things" so that her life was not completely oriented around the bar: "Waking up in the afternoon, going to work, drinking at work, going home, passing out, waking up." By making the individual worker accountable, the market is not responsible for outcomes experienced by the individual.

Precarious conditions of *immaterial labour* are too easily couched in autonomy, flexibility, and freedom in decision making, where the individual is held accountable for such precarious labour market conditions as irregular or casual hours; meagre contracts, if any at all; increased responsibility for the individual worker to make their own decisions; and the growth of competition in job-seeking brought about by processes of globalisation and human mobility. Lazzarato (2006) explains the valorisation of life as largely blinded by the autonomy and the individualism that *immaterial labourers* are awarded through the varying degrees of responsibility afforded to them in decision making. Like I explored in Chapter 1, this rampant hyper-individualism is often referred to through the political frame of neoliberalism; an ideology based on laissez faire capitalism—a 'let the markets be' approach to governance—where the individual is solely responsible, and rewarded, for prevailing amidst chaotic and competitive socio-economic conditions (Silva 2013). *Immaterial labourers* are encouraged to be autonomous at work—they are not governed by the traditional vertical division of labour and Taylorist precision of scientific management on the assembly line (Hardt & Negri 2000; Lazzarato 2006). The skills that are increasingly required of postmodern workers are abstract; they are a "form-of-life" that often go unaccounted for (Gill & Pratt 2008; Hardt 1999, p. 98). Benjamin Snyder (2016, p. 214) describes the glorification of flexibility and autonomy as a type of "Faustian bargain with the working self". Snyder (2016) describes the way contemporary workers are enticed to give up all traditional notions of predictability, standardisation, and centralisation, in exchange for being granted the flexibility and freedom to carve out a unique path for themselves. But this sacrifice comes at a cost to the workers inasmuch as "the temporality of life becomes governed by work" accordingly

(Gill & Pratt 2008, p. 17; Gregg 2009). Snyder (2016, p. 214) suggests sustainability is of critical importance in looking beyond this *disruption culture*, in that workers challenge "the instability of capitalist time", given that its current accelerated, time-consuming, autonomous, and obsessive provocations are inevitably unsustainable.

Affective capitalism is motored by the notion that temporal joy increases the body's desire to continue that feeling of pleasure, ontologically gripping the body's capacity to act on pleasure, pain, and 'the moment'. That workers were seduced by the venues in which they worked, and that this helped to generate value in the 'hip' economy, is illustrative of the notion that feelings are triggered *situationally*, and become internalised to form more *contextual* and performed filters of emotion (Massumi 2002). Emotions are embodied and intentional states, whereas affects are in a constant state of transformation and becoming and, in this way, they are pre-individual and happen prior to conscious perception (Seigworth & Gregg 2010, p. 2). Workers appeared to 'pay the price', so to speak, for short-term gratifications associated with the job based on their level of personal investment in the 'hip' economy in which they were employed. Crucially, their personal investment resulting from feeling transient pleasures further characterises the 'affected labourer'—whose degree of appreciation and respect for the venue, and its accompanying lifestyle, determines their level of personal investment in it. Workers' forfeiting of stable desires follows a personal investment in the venue they work at, while at the same time the market derives surplus value from the investment of 'affected labourers' in the generation of value. It is the silent process of workers being moved and touched in ecologies of interaction; investing; and buying in to the venue and lifestyle that helps to generate value in 'hip' economies.

Rather than conceptualising interactions between workers and consumers in terms of a logic of exchange, the interactional ecologies of transparency, detachment, and ephemerality, in this research, functioned on a multidimensional plane that was hinged upon workers, customers, employers, and commentators collectively engaging as 'players', or 'users', in their combined creation of the assemblage's vibe—and its potential to generate value. This multidimensional plane, moreover, existed through the stripping away of traditional notions of *emotional labour* and performed notions of service, in order to produce organic, honest, and authentic meaning for those who worked in the precarious hospitality industry (Hochschild 1983). While short-lived as they happened, encounters materialised into forces that confronted individuals and determined their 'choices' and, in this way, the process of seducing 'affected labourers' existed in excess to the material commodities they enlarged and hence moved according to their own ecologies, rather than the ethics of capitalism. Moreover, the interactional ecologies of transparency, detachment, and temporality operated in terms of how individual 'players' could best maximise pleasure and minimise pain (Spinoza 1996).

Affect *is* 'the moment': it is strongest in the present. Feeling is the "thisness" of everyday life and, following Massumi (2015, pp. 152–153), it is the crucial instant affects form that provides "the invitational opening for a rationality to get its hooks into the flesh" (Seigworth & Gregg 2010, p. 3). Capitalising on feeling in 'the moment' in precarious times is hegemonic, because in 'the moment' affect is "the domain of 'mere' feeling. It represents the vulnerability of the individual to larger societal forces. Power hooks into the individual through feeling, and then pulls the strings that lead the individual into deluded acquiescence to its assigned role" (Massumi 2015, p. 153). Acknowledging our simultaneous vulnerability and reliance upon affects amidst the constant shocks of postmodern culture, or *disruption culture*—in the everyday "life of the mind" and the capitalist context—presents a sustainable vector for dealing with the precarious contemporary experience (Snyder 2016; Virno 2004, p. 49). Following Massumi (2015, p. 19):

> There's like a population or swarm of potential ways of affecting or being affected that follows along as we move through life. We always have a vague sense that they're there. That vague sense of potential, we call it our "freedom", and defend it fiercely.

As immaterial production continues to grow in postmodernity—and capitalise on shock-factor reactions in 'the moment'—the significance and 'nature' of feeling is critical and worthy of meaningful consideration in formulating economies of desire.

Affects represent "a sense of push in the world" (Thrift 2004, p. 64). Affect is pre-individual and defined by its transformational, fleeting, and collaborative function that is contingent upon the situation in which it arises (Clough et. al 2007). This means that the challenge amidst the chaotic world of affective encounters is to analyse the way feeling gathers and governs individuals (Brown & Stenner 2001; Sharp 2007). By developing Hochschild's (1983) work on the deep personal implications of directing feelings inwardly in order to do the job—what she terms *emotional labour*—the more subtle, aesthetic, atmospheric, and visceral elements that help to shape workers' perceptions of their job and self are illuminated. In doing so, this research renegotiates the idea that underpins both Hochschild's (1983) concept of *emotional labour* and Hardt and Negri's (2000) concept of *affective labour*: that labour is designed by an employer, performed by a worker, and consumed by a demanding customer. I propose, rather, that 'affected labour' is a product 'of the moment', and the result of forces of encounter (affect) between workers, customers, employers, and the atmospheric spaces in which the labour takes place; the worker is *not* the sole provider and performer of the product. Where the language of *emotional and affective labour* accentuates the worker as a performer who is providing for a customer—first and foremost *doing something for someone else*—the subtle shift in emphasis from affect*ing* to affect*ed* communicates the essence of this type of labour in 'hip' economies more broadly, that is, work concerned with input (Hardt & Negri 2000; Hochschild 1983). Moreover, this input-driven nature of the job—of being affected—further blurs the lines between life and labour.

Summary

Workers were significantly less free to detach from short-term pleasurable affects, which held greater control over them. Most workers felt stuck in an industry which fulfilled many of their short-term desires, often at the expense of their long-term ones. The intensity of short-term and positive pleasures prompted many workers to personally invest in their workplace (and employers), sacrificing to varying degrees such long-term desires as to get out of the industry altogether. Temporal benefits like flexible hours, low responsibility, a social platform, or a place to embody and exteriorise, if not pastiche an 'identity', affected workers much more. Such short-term benefits of 'affected labour', and the temporality embedded in *Toyota-ist* production more generally, mirror the 'nature' of affect as "this-ness", "fleeting", and momentary (Hardt 1999; Seigworth & Gregg 2010, p. 3). This was illustrated very clearly in a statement Sam made:

> I think you think to yourself, "Oh, I'm not going to be doing this forever." Maybe that kind of helps, or, "I've really got to get out of this." But I've felt like that a lot, and then come the next day I'll have a really nice day and I'm like, "Oh, this is alright. I could do this for a while longer."

Even though the majority of the workers' encounters with patrons were muted, where the workers had learned to detach and often ridicule the interaction according to common experiences with "feeling like crap", it was the intensity of spontaneously feeling seemingly authentic joy in the short term that resonated with workers significantly more (Jasper). While joy was less frequent, it was qualitatively more consequential. Illuminatingly, in almost every conversation I had workers presented beautifully colourful and romantic depictions of a job, and world, that they ultimately did not want to be in. So, the widely felt fulfilment of short-term desires, despite continued feelings of insecurity and precariousness around the industry's limited vocational trajectory, meant workers were personally investing in, or buying into, the economy of short-term pleasures that potentially exploits them.

Reference list

Brown, SD & Stenner, P 2001, 'Being Affected: Spinoza and the Psychology of Emotion', *International Journal of Group Tensions*, vol. 30, no. 1, pp. 81–104.

Clough, PT, Goldberg, G, Schiff, R, Weeks, A & Wilse, C 2007, 'Notes Towards a Theory of Affect-Itself', *Ephemera: Theory & Politics in Organization*, vol. 7, no. 1, pp. 60–77.

Gill, R & Pratt, A 2008, 'In the Social Factory? Immaterial Labour, Precariousness and Cultural Work', *Theory, Culture & Society*, vol. 25, no. 7–8, pp. 1–30.

Gregg, M 2009, 'Learning to (Love) Labour: Production Cultures and The Affective Turn', *Communication and Critical/Cultural Studies*, vol. 6, no. 2, pp. 209–214.

Hardt, M 1999, 'Affective Labor', *boundary 2*, vol. 26, no. 2, pp. 89–100.

Hardt, M 2007, 'What Affects Are Good For', *The Affective Turn: Theorizing the Social*, eds. PT Clough & J Halley, Duke University Press, Durham & London.

Hardt, M & Negri, A 2000, *Empire*, Harvard University Press, Cambridge.

Hardt, M & Negri, A 2004, *Multitude: War and Democracy in the Age of Empire*, Penguin Press, New York.

Hochschild, AR 1983, *The Managed Heart: Commercialization of Human Feeling*, University of California Press, Berkeley & Los Angeles.

Lazzarato, M 2006, 'Immaterial Labor', trans. P Colilli & E Emory in *Radical Thought in Italy: A Potential Politics*, eds. M Hardt & P Virno, University of Minnesota Press, Minneapolis, pp. 132–147.

Lloyd, A 2012, 'Working to Live, Not Living to Work: Work, Leisure and Youth Identity Among Call Centre Workers in North East England', *Current Sociology*, vol. 60, no. 5, pp. 619–635.

Massumi, B 2002, *Parables for the Virtual*, Duke University Press, Durham & London.

Massumi, B 2015, *The Politics of Affect*, Polity, Cambridge, Oxford & Boston.

Seigworth, GJ & Gregg, M (eds.) 2010, 'An Inventory of Shimmers', *The Affect Theory Reader*, Duke University Press, Durham & London, pp. 1–25.

Sharp, H 2007, 'The Force of Ideas in Spinoza', *Political Theory*, vol. 35, no. 6, pp. 732–755.

Silva, J 2013, *Coming Up Short: Working-Class Adulthood in an Age of Uncertainty*, Oxford University Press, New York.

Snyder, B 2016, *The Disrupted Workplace: Time and the Moral Order of Flexible Capitalism*, Oxford University Press, New York.

Spinoza, B 1996, *The Ethics*, trans. E Curley, Penguin Group, London.

Thrift, N 2004, 'Intensities of Feeling: Towards a Spatial Politics of Affect', *Geografiska Annaler*, Series B, vol. 86, no. 1, pp. 57–78.

Tsianos, V & Papadopoulos, D 2006, 'Precarity: A Savage Journey to the Heart of Embodied Capitalism', *Transversal Journal*. Available from: http://eipcp.net/trans versal/1106/tsianospapadopoulos/en [29 July 2014].

Virno, P 2004, *The Grammar of the Multitude: For an Analysis of Contemporary Forms of Life*, MIT Press, Cambridge & London.

6 The 'hip' gentrification of precarious work

I recall, vividly, a conversation I had with an inspiring teacher a few weeks prior to my departure for Melbourne to commence doctoral study. We spoke of the joys of teaching and learning together, and he told me, "When you have a good teacher, when you get to experience that, you feel some kind of a duty to pass it on—to carry it on." When one is touched by an educator they have a greater power to act, learn, and ultimately go on to affect others. And, in the same way, if the educator is not moved by their students, the learning atmosphere, and the teaching content, how could they possibly be expected to infect students with passion and intrigue? In Pablo Picasso's self-portrait *Au Lapin Agile* (1905) the artist is in a bar, dressed in a Harlequin costume with a morose or lonely expression on his face, standing slouched over the bar leaner next to a fashionable, bourgeois patron. That night, Picasso found an admirer of his work in the bar and, on his way home, shot his pistol into the air, moved by the sheer joy of finding an interpreter and follower of his work (Wagner 2013/14). Affecting and being affected are built into everyday life encounters between bodies and objects (both immaterial and material) and each time they occur they bring a margin for change: an opening for an experiential transformation in the body (Massumi 2015a). The constancy of affecting and being affected is both part of capitalism and, yet, happens irrespectively of it. In this way, affects are ontological, or "transversal" because they switch between social domains at great speeds, transgressing the categorical boundaries of many traditional social spheres (Massumi 1995, p. 107). In Massumi's words, affect "is beyond infrastructural, it is everywhere, in effect" (1995, pp. 106–107).

Work that produces immaterial goods and services should be considered as dependent upon labourers being joyfully moved by the experience, interaction, brand, atmosphere/workplace, and employers. The job of baristas and bartenders, in this research, was defined by how the productive process impacted individual workers and, in doing so, how it determined their longevity and commitment to doing the job well, or not, as active 'players' in the creation and potential success of the product. Workers' being moved shaped the value of the service they gave, induced their loyalty toward the company they worked for, and encouraged their communication of the brand's vibe according to interactional ecologies situated in a field of emergence. The ecologies of interaction—transparency, detachment, and ephemerality—produced such qualities as a sense of organic and authentic exchange, rather than a forced and scripted rendition of service; transparency around what the labour involved (hipster hospitality); pastiche and parody of the role; a certain type of freedom and surrendering of a serious self; and liberation from the mainstream white- and blue-collar—rhythmic nine-to-five—labour market, through the flexibility and autonomy allowed by the job. Instead of consciously imputing emotion onto feeling, for example through *deep* and *surface* acting, 'hip' economies extract value from the authentic and intuitively-felt spontaneity of *production in 'the moment'* (Hochschild 1983). If workers were affected positively they would very likely affect the customer back, by providing better service and personally investing in the brand/venue that they were seduced through. Rather than the notion that 'the customer is always right', café and bar assemblages create seductive atmospheres that take the emphasis away from five-star renditions of service, in favour of a more genuine approach to the interactional labour, and in accordance with the well-documented fracturing and precariousness that defines the postmodern or neoliberal experience (see Beck 1992; Boltanski & Chiapello 2007; Giddens 1991; Hardt & Negri 2000; Lasch 1979; Lyotard 1984; Sennett 1998; Silva 2013; Snyder 2016).

The atmospheres and personal envisions formed within venues—and reproduced by individual engaged 'players' colliding—happened on a shared plane of relations, rather than a transactional logic of exchange. If workers were seduced, and moved by pleasure, they would likely do a good job, by giving their customer better service, embodying the venue's image, and personally investing in the venue that they work. Correspondingly, if the customer wasn't seduced by the venue, they likely wouldn't return—as is expressed in the high turnover of hospitality ventures in Melbourne. The businesses, too, needed to be moved by their customers; they were reliant upon the *production cultures* that they could engender, so as to reinforce their cultural relevancy and upbeat feel (Gregg 2009). Immaterial production is, as Jasper suggested, like running on a treadmill that never stops; it is motored by the push to survive constant possibilities of irrelevancy. Henceforth, the ephemerality of such 'hip' industries as Melbourne's hospitality produces up-to-date trends that shape, and are shaped by, popular culture. Market 'rationality' and profitability are calculated by momentarily freezing certain affective states in reactionary zones that are in a constant state of emergence and becoming (Massumi 2015b). Sensorial stimulation and processes of seduction in affective capitalism, as production endlessly strives for refinement in order to keep up, moves all 'players' who are persuaded by one another in the production process. Being affected functions according to its own interactional ecology—in response to the situation in which it arises—rather than according to an isolated logic of exchange or traditional capitalist ethics like 'service with a smile'. In a way, no one is really in control of the service encounter, and this is part of what gives the service encounter, worker, atmosphere, and product a hipster quality: inhospitable and hyperreal hospitality.

Unlike the service boom of the 1980s and 1990s, in order to generate value in 'hip' postmodern economies, it is not enough to perform corny or put-on service—it won't be affective, it won't vibe (Hochschild 1983). Rather, 'hip' value engenders feelings in *all* of the subjects involved in the collective generation of brand value, through interacting with it on the spot in zones of aesthetical and atmospheric intensity and shock factor. Inducing customers into feeling a certain way forms a dynamic currency that transgresses the traditional transactional exchange, in a multidimensional plane of relations between workers, employers, consumers, commentators, and the atmospheres of the assemblages. The momentary force of the workers' first encounter with their customer inevitably touched them, and they used the feeling, born out of the encounter, as a gauge in their production of service thereafter.

Because workers faced an unpredictable patronage so constantly they were encouraged to manage transactional relationships in 'the moment', which is an embedded part of postmodern or *Toyota-ist* production, more generally, and under which immaterial surplus thrives (Hardt 1999; Hochschild 1983). Think of the recent media exposure of airplane hosts and hostesses who have been filmed abusing airplane passengers: the erosion of five-star service in postmodern work happens because the workers' job, albeit often unconsciously, is to *act in 'the moment' and practice transparency*. For a café culture built on otherworldly aesthetic spaces, the typical style of service in Melbourne is of a remarkably muted quality. While, as Jess explained, the latte art in the cafés of New York City pales in comparison to Melbourne's, I wonder whether styles of service in America are following Melbourne's 'hip' trends? I'm curious as to whether the aesthetical shock-factor quality of cafés and bars in America is as intense as it is in Melbourne. The *mood economy*—in its sensorial intensity—is built on the idea that in the uncontrollable and felt moment, one's strength at arranging the reaction determines the type of response given (Silva 2013; Spinoza 1996). This is perhaps why the gauging work performed is something of a distillation method that workers relied upon for approaching their service with the unpredictable customer. As Arthur pointed out, "You have to feel your crowd."

Most workers felt trapped in an industry which fulfilled many of their short-term desires, often at the expense of their long-term ones, prompting many to personally invest in the venue, sacrificing to varying degrees such long-term desires as getting out of the industry altogether. Short-term benefits—like flexible hours, low responsibility, a social platform, or a place to embody and exteriorise, if not pastiche an identity—touched them considerably more in accord with the 'nature' of affect as most physically intense when positive and temporal (Hardt 1999; Seigworth & Gregg 2010, p. 3). Despite the fact that the majority of workers' encounters with patrons were muted, where they learnt to detach and often ridicule and pastiche the interaction according to their common experiences with negative affect, it was the intensity of positive short-term feelings that resonated with them significantly more. While pleasure was less frequent, it was more consequential. Illuminatingly, most workers expressed beautifully colourful and romantic depictions of a job, and world, that they ultimately did not want to be in. Despite continued feelings of insecurity and precariousness around the industry's limited vocational trajectory, the widely-felt fulfilment of short-term desires lead them to buy into the economy of short-term pleasures that seems to mask the precarious experience.

The force of 'the moment', in terms of both production in the new economy as well as in the ethics of affect, presents an exploitative threat through the unpredictable charge feelings have on impressionable and nostalgic bodies. Affect *exists* as the body's vulnerability to 'the moment': it is most impactful on a temporal plane (Seigworth & Gregg 2010). This is precisely why affective production freezes and capitalises on 'the moment' through manipulating "the domain of 'mere' feeling" (Massumi 2015a, p. 153). When workers are seduced they are malleable assets to a company, yet their heightened productivity, which benefits their employers and the products that they sell, is not recognised through a traditional principle of equivalence in the labour market—other than (probably) getting them the job in the first place. In Theresa Cowan and Jasmine Rault's (2014) bold article 'The Labour of Being Studied in a Free Love Economy', the authors explore the artistic and academic industries as sites with affective currencies. Examples like the web 2.0, the common sentiment of doing "what we love", and the currency of goodwill, illuminate capitalism's reliance on "labours of love", and the resultant inequality of affective resource distribution, given that the resource primarily utilised by *immaterial labour* is the mind (Cowan & Rault 2014, p. 473). The authors call for an acknowledgment, or free market, within the capitalist context that can account for the collaborative nature of the *free love economy*, given today's well-camouflaged and heavy reliance on "labours of love" (Cowan & Rault 2014, p. 473).

Does widespread precariousness relate to the ascendancy of 'affected labour'? In many ways, contemporary workers are 'users', too, subscribing to their workplace and its products, affects, interactions, vibes, aesthetics, etc., and subtly being bound to the workplace and job. Rather than conceptualising *user experience* solely in terms of the consumer's experience, what if the worker, too, was recognised as an active 'user', engaged in the production of (immaterial) value? What would be the secondary and tangential consequences of this focus on the 'affected labourer' for thinking about work in the postmodern? The precarious work of baristas and bartenders in this book was made 'hip' through the force of 'the moment', which rendered traditional, premeditated, Taylorist production principles as largely redundant in the new work experience (Hardt & Negri 2000). The ecologies of interaction were the outcome of the significant weight placed on *spontaneous impact* induced collectively—among *affected* customers, businesses, and, most pressingly, workers themselves. Which other 'hip' industries are prevailing, and do they, too, require the worker be seduced in their generating of surplus value? Popular and recognisable new businesses that capitalise on engaging their workers (as 'users') and affectively enlarging their products, including Uber, Airbnb, and Air Tasker, as well as part-time, temporary, gig work, and flexible work more generally, are paradoxically both highly unstable and insecure forms of work that, at the same time, present potentially 'hip' and seductive options. To what extent, then, does 'affected labour' apply to the broader, precarious new economy? Moreover, are such unstable working conditions in the new work experience made possible through the affective refurbishment of 'dirty work'?

The interactional ecologies, in this research, were an outcome of workers being moved against the script and according to the strength of momentary pleasures and, in in this way, their 'affected labour' made low-paid and precarious 'dirty work' more artful and seductive. The staff were touched in uncontrollable ways by the 'nature' of their working with—and living in—'the moment' (Spinoza 1996; Tsianos & Papadopoulos 2006). The rational-actor model that defines neoliberalism, where individuals feel accountable and solely responsible for changing the structural failures that constrain them, doesn't account for the irrationality and compulsion of even our most controlled selves (Silva 2013). Indeed, Massumi (2015b, p. 2) describes "rational" economics today as "a division of the affective arts", because economists pause specific moments of intense feeling—and replicate them—in a cyclical type of "mood ring". Affect-based industries capitalise on 'the moment' in precarious times; where little is foreseeable, little is guaranteed. Indeed, "the rise of the precariat" is increasingly a reality for those working in formally white-collar and upscale jobs: rising temporary labour, mass casualisation, and the *gig economy* are labour-market trends affecting those at the top of the labour-market hierarchy too (Johnson 2017). The central issue here that is worth critical attention is that the volatility of contemporary labour-market conditions, and the potential for mass disenfranchisement, also tempts with seductive options for those postmodern individuals pursuing authenticity—through autonomy, creative expression, detachment, flexible hours, pleasurable affects, triviality, transparency, and thinking on the spot or 'being present'—in (understandably) longing "for the lost innocence of spontaneous feeling" (Lasch 1979, p. 93).

Reference list

Beck, U 1992, *Risk Society: Towards a New Modernity*, trans. M Ritter, Sage, Los Angeles.

Boltanski, L & Chiapello, E 2007, *The New Spirit of Capitalism*, trans. G Elliot, Verso, New York.

Cowan, TL & Rault, J 2014, 'The Labor of Being Studied in a Free Love Economy', *Ephemera: Theory & Politics in Organization*, vol. 14, no. 3, pp. 471–488.

Giddens, A 1991, *Modernity and Self-Identity*, Stanford University Press, Palo Alto.

Gregg, M 2009, 'Learning to (Love) Labour: Production Cultures and The Affective Turn', *Communication and Critical/Cultural Studies*, vol. 6, no. 2, pp. 209–214.

Hardt, M 1999, 'Affective Labor', *boundary 2*, vol. 26, no. 2, pp. 89–100.

Hardt, M & Negri, A 2000, *Empire*, Harvard University Press, Cambridge.

Hochschild, AR 1983, *The Managed Heart: Commercialization of Human Feeling*, University of California Press, Berkeley & Los Angeles.

Johnson, N 2017, *The Rise of the Precariat*. Available at: http://economia.icaew.com/en/features/june-2017/the-rise-of-the-precariat [6 October 2017].

Lasch, C 1979, *The Culture of Narcissism: American Life in an Age of Diminishing Expectations*, George J. McLeod, Toronto.

Lyotard, JF 1984, *The Postmodern Condition: A Report on Knowledge*, University of Minnesota Press, Minneapolis.

Massumi, B 1995, 'The Autonomy of Affect', *Cultural Critique*, Spring, no. 31, pp. 83–109.

Massumi, B 2015a, *The Politics of Affect*, Polity, Cambridge, Oxford & Boston.

Massumi, B 2015b, *The Power at the End of the Economy*, Duke University Press, Durham & London.

Seigworth, GJ & Gregg, M (eds.) 2010, 'An Inventory of Shimmers', *The Affect Theory Reader*, Duke University Press, Durham & London, pp. 1–25.

Sennett, R 1998, *The Corrosion of Character: The Personal Consequences of Work in the New Capitalism*, WW Norton & Company, New York.

Silva, J 2013, *Coming up Short: Working-Class Adulthood in an Age of Uncertainty*, Oxford University Press, New York.

Snyder, B 2016, *The Disrupted Workplace: Time and the Moral Order of Flexible Capitalism*, Oxford University Press, New York.

Spinoza, B 1996, *The Ethics*, trans. E Curley, Penguin Group, London.

Tsianos, V & Papadopoulos, D 2006, 'Precarity: A Savage Journey to the Heart of Embodied Capitalism', *Transversal Journal*. Available from: http://eipcp.net/transversal/1106/tsianospapadopoulos/en [29 July 2014].

Wagner, T 2013/14, 'Destiny 1913', *032c*, 25th Issue, Berlin, Winter, pp. 68–76.

Appendix
Research methodology

Identifying the research field

In identifying the venues that I wished to engage in the research, I approached those that represented the internationally renowned hospitality culture. These I found located in Melbourne's inner suburbs, especially in the inner north of the city. Part of my intrigue with this particular field site was the marked differences between high-end venues, particularly within the inner northern suburbs where capital was deliberately affective, and those in the outer suburbs of the city that cultivated more traditional and localised ethics like 'service with a smile' or suburban bakeries, for example, that catered to communities of diasporas. Yet a cup of coffee or a beer costs roughly the same price, irrespective of the venue's luxury or non-luxury status. Moreover, venues located in the inner suburbs of the city represented the café and bar industries' international reputation, as Melbourne increasingly undergoes gentrification and capitalism chases the city's suburban sprawl.

During early research planning, I spent time looking through the two prominent Melbourne lifestyle websites: Broadsheet and Three Thousand, as well as the annual *Melbourne Good Food Guide*. Frequently, I walked around the city gauging the culture I had identified as being unique because I was new to the city, having arrived from New Zealand to commence my PhD candidature. In this way, I was initially the outsider, de-familiarised and able to see the distinctiveness of Melbourne hospitality. In fact, before I moved to Melbourne I had lived in Wellington, which, despite an estimated population of 203,800 (Statistics New Zealand 2013), has more cafés per capita than any other city in the world! During my years of undergraduate study in Wellington, I had worked part-time in several different cafés and so was well acquainted with café culture. Nevertheless, in Melbourne I was confronted with a very different scene that, as an outsider, seemed strikingly professionalised and aesthetically and atmospherically much more intense than anything I had seen in Wellington. Even something as simple, for example, as the fact that baristas in some venues wore fashionable full-length aprons made out of denim, or with leather straps or embroidery and so on, stood out to me as distinctive, perhaps even unique, to the city's hospitality culture.

The data presented in this research was drawn from ten cafés and bars, which, according to their international representation and intensity of affect, I have described as 'hip'. Half of the venues were bars and half were cafés, located in the CBD, Collingwood, Fitzroy, Fitzroy North, Northcote, North Melbourne, and South Melbourne. All of the venues have been featured in such leading Melbourne lifestyle websites as Broadsheet and Three Thousand.

Entering the field: beginning observation

After all baristas and bartenders who worked in the selected venues had signed and returned their consent forms, and I had arranged a rough plan with each manager as to when I would be coming in to their venue, I began fieldwork. I commenced with observation, which is regarded as the mainstay of the ethnographic project—that is, to see another's world through their eyes (Madden 2010). More specifically, I used *reactive observation*, meaning that the population were aware of me watching them and were open to interacting with me in response to elements of the research project (Davies 2008). The other approach commonly used by ethnographers is *participant observation*, where the researcher is fully immersed in the life of the population in whom they are interested. As such, their position as researcher is quickly forgotten given their high involvement in undertaking the same tasks and lifestyle as the population they are observing. The reality of undertaking fieldwork in 'hip' Melbourne hospitality is that it is commercial, rendering it ethically problematic to fully participate in the field and with the bar and café staff during trading hours, and thus running the risk of damaging the venue's productivity and profits. To negotiate the absence of a firsthand account by my use of *reactive observation*, I also worked in a high-profile coffee shop in the CBD to deepen my insights, not to use as data per se but to use reflexively as material for a personal journal (Davies 2008). In this journal, I wrote entries after my shifts at the café, which were largely oriented around my feelings at the time and my relationships with colleagues and the café's clientele. This was important because, pace Raymond Madden (2010, p. 161, emphasis in original), "it is *ethnographers*, not ethnographies, who need to take responsibility for the shape and purpose of ethnographic stories".

I spent time in the field over four, sometimes five, days per week—in the cafés during the day, from 10am to 1pm, or 2pm to 5pm—and following which I conducted observations in bars during the evening in two time slots, from 6pm to 9pm, or 10pm to midnight. I visited venues in a different order each day, so that I was able to see the range of affective atmospheres within each venue over the course of the week. For example, I observed the bar in Collingwood on a Saturday night, when it was packed, as well as on a Wednesday night, in the middle of winter, when customers were scarce. The managers of the venues were generous in allowing me to sit and observe during their busiest business hours. I explained during the recruitment process that I would be happy to work around their busy times, but every manager who took part in the research was happy for me to be there when it was busiest, giving me richer insights into aspects of their jobs. I took a notebook into the venue, sat either at the bar or near the till in the cafés, and scribbled notes based on what I saw. During early stages of observation, I was initially drawn to describing the venues' atmospheres and various aesthetic dimensions. But the looser my wrist grew and the more accustomed I became with the different venues, the participants, and the experience of doing fieldwork more generally, the freer and more able I felt to record specific dialogue that I overheard, or to describe specific collisions and affects.

Often, while observing, I pretended I had never been into a café or bar in my life, as if I were from another planet, and took note of what I saw in such a frame of mind, akin to the process that Zygmunt Bauman and Tim May (2001, p. 15) describe as "de-familiarizing the familiar". As I did this, I wrote individual vignettes for each venue as unrestrained and informal descriptions, based on my initial affected judgment of the venue. This was an important aspect of my practice that informed my reflexivity in the field, given that I myself was affected while I was reporting on affects. In this way, I could record the affects I personally encountered, in order to remember the specific ways venues affected me, which proved useful as I reflected on these notes. While I could record my personal emotions and reactions over the course of the fieldwork, with time I was able to work my written emotional responses into the broader data set without letting my emotional subjectivity interfere with the data. When it was quiet at the venues, workers often interacted with me as I observed their place of work. This was especially true in the bars, since I was sitting within arm's reach of the bartenders. I often noted down our informal conversations during the night, and these became insightful parts of my data. Workers opened up on the job, in the platform the venue put them on, and their insights intensified as a result. This I discuss in detail in Chapter 5. Given the fleeting, almost manic, nature of café and bar spaces, especially when they were busiest, as well as the resultant scribbly observations I wrote—often recorded in the midst of highly transient situations—I was driven to reread my notes and study any diagrams I had mapped out during the tram rides back home. Thus, if any of my notes were unreadable I was able to rewrite and develop them in the context of very recent recollections. At the end of each week, I typed up the notes and scribbles that had accumulated in my notebook. This helped to facilitate my own exploration of the critical theory I was reading, such that I could analyse and push further the intersections between theory and my empirical observations as I developed these insights across the fieldwork period.

Beginning interviews

I interviewed twenty employees across the ten venues. Ten of these identified as female and ten as male. Interviewees gave me their cell phone numbers, following which I called them to organise a place and time to meet. Usually this was at the venue where they worked, but three of the interviews were conducted at other hospitality venues for practical reasons. All interviews took place outside employees' formal working hours, either before or after their shifts. During the year before fieldwork, when I was collecting theoretical material and developing my research objectives, I compiled a list of potential questions. These became the basis for the interview questions I used with café and bar staff, and were oriented around what I saw as missing in the literature, together with some issues addressed in critiques of the literature. I refined the initial interview questions to align them with the themes that were emerging from my observations and notetaking, and thus compiled a new list of twenty open-ended questions. For example, I noticed the theme of *detachment* emerging during the early stages of observation in that some workers seemed remarkably muted in their expressions toward their clientele. This theme was integrated into one of my interview questions, which was: *Do you have any specific techniques for dealing with customers?*

I began each interview with introductory questions about the interviewee's biography and personal narrative: *How long have you worked here? Is this your only job? How many hours do you work on average per week? What did you do for work before this job? Are you paid fairly?* Once we were familiar with each other, I moved onto such open-ended questions as: *What is Melbourne hospitality to you? Do you feel like you have freedom in your job? What is a good day and what is a bad day? Are you aware of being watched by customers while you are working? Do you want to continue working in your current job, and the industry more generally?* And as I mentioned earlier: *Do you have any specific techniques for dealing with customers?* I found, after becoming familiar with the interviewee early in the interview, that asking direct rather than ambiguous questions generated unique responses because the question was not carrying with it any hints of preconceived answers. For example, when I asked one interviewee what his plans were, he explained that while he did want to continue working at the venue he did *not* want to work in hospitality. His answer led him to tell me about the fundamental tension he felt bar staff faced between short- and long-term desires, which we spent some time discussing as my interview questions moved away from the framework of the original interview schedule. I recorded all interviews on my iPhone, and stored them electronically on my computer, so that throughout the year of fieldwork I could listen to them on my iPhone, as I walked around the city.

Leaving the field: data analysis

Once I had conducted the twenty interviews, I compiled my typed observational field notes into one document for each venue, and printed and reread them to begin the data analysis process. I used *thematic analysis* to interpret the data, which is a strategy that identifies and induces themes by categorising the field notes, personal anecdotes, and interview recordings. By utilising an *inductive* approach, I was able to let the data speak to me, rather than using a *deductive* approach that either confirms or denies the hypotheses that are imputed from the data before analysis. I began first by *open coding* my observation transcripts where, through rereading them, sets of categories emerged, each with their own properties or subthemes (Ezzy 2002). My first *open code* generated eleven broad categories, each with seven dimensions attached to that category. These categories were: *Job, Craftsman, Social platform/private self, Show/pantomime/parody, Intimacy against assembly line, Gauging ties, Influences on service, Reality affirmations,*

Affect/contagion, Capitalising on affect, and *Hospitality codes.* Thus, the eleven categories that emerged from my *open code* were very broad in terms of their meaning and reach. For example, the category named *Influences on service* encapsulated eight subthemes as follows: *Company ethics, Individually articulated work, Customer, The meaning of service (hospitality without hospitableness), Service as more holistic, Service as experience (use-value), Service as not hidden,* and *Affect as opposed to service.* In other words, I was covering broad conceptual terrain in the early stages of *open coding,* which allowed me to justify the breadth of observation notes I had accumulated.

Next, I began *axial coding,* where after rereading the observation transcripts that were organised around the eleven categories and subcategories I integrated them into fewer central categories; this is a process of condensing relationships between dimensions (Ezzy 2002). For example, I found that four of the categories from the *open coding—Show/pantomime/parody, Intimacy against assembly line, Individually articulated work,* and *Influences on service—*all pointed to the nature of *affective labour,* as well as the hegemonic element within the work. Thus, *the nature of affective labour as opposed to other forms of labour, namely its hegemonic form,* became a core category that comprised the subcategories I mentioned above. At the end of *axial coding,* the eleven themes were collapsed into four thematic categories, which covered the core themes within the data sample, each with six or seven dimensions. These themes emerged when I saw new relationships between categories and subcategories, in the process of reorganisation. The four core categories were:

a)   The nature of *affective labour* as opposed to other forms of labour, namely its hegemonic form;
b)   The mechanisms of affect and emotional contagion;
c)   How affect becomes commodified; and
d)   The implications of funnelling behaviour on the labour market.

I then used these categories as the basis for my *thematic analysis* of the recorded interviews. I began the analysis by listening to each interview and noting down core variables that made up each participant's biography. For example, I noted their age, how long they had worked in hospitality and the specific venue, any other work they did, and so on. These functioned like individual biographies to reference throughout the analysis and writing phases, so that I could situate each interviewee's voice in the framework of their individual identity and personal narrative. One participant, for example, had walked out on the job a week prior to our interview over a dispute with his manager. While our conversation was deep, it nevertheless possessed overtones of resentment and arrogance, which I needed to situate in the broader framework of this participant's mind and personal situation in my interpretation of his interview transcript. I then went through each interview, noting every part that covered some aspect of the four *axial codes* and their subcategories, generated from the observation scripts. This did not produce forced linking-up of themes because the *axial codes* were broad enough to cover the majority of the content in both the observation and interview transcripts. I also had a separate document for other parts of the interviews that were discerning but did not fit into the *axial coding* categories and their properties. I then integrated into one document the interview and observation excerpts according to the four themes, together with relevant personal anecdotes from my journal.

I then returned to the neighbourhoods of literature that I addressed in the previous chapter, which I had studied during the first year of my research. I reacquainted myself with the important theoretical texts, and positioned the ethnographic data according to its place in the larger critical picture. This prepared me to begin the final *selective coding*, where I was able to identify the core *story* generated by the *axial coding* (Ezzy 2002). To do this, I looked closely at the causal and sequential relationships between dimensions and other dimensions, or categories and dimensions, so that a narrative emerged. I imagined I was telling someone, step by step, what the data was saying, and this became a story with eighteen points, each point only one or two sentences. The story became the framework for *selective coding*, wherein I broke the eighteen-part story down into four parts, which functioned as separate chapters. The four parts were: *The strength of positive affect, Affected service, Reality affirmation*, and *Temporality*, and each category had four or five properties. For example, after selective coding, the initial *open coding* category named *Influences on service* developed into more of a narrative, which was named *Affected service*. Where the original category's dimensions had included *Company ethics, Individually articulated, Customer, The meaning of service (hospitality without hospitality), Service as more holistic, Service as experience (use-value), Service as not hidden*, and *Affect as opposed to service*, after *selective coding* these became:

a)   Employees moderate affect as a personal coping strategy;
b)   This becomes part of the service they give;
c)   And this is largely because of the unpredictability of people;
d)   Thus, the staff are occupationally and affectively reflexive;
e)   Which they defend through their undisguised show of labour; and
f)   So, customers (ideally) fit in to the venue.

Since completing my final *selective code*, the story into which I had organised my data changed, because, like Laurel Richardson and Elizabeth Adams St. Pierre have posited, "writing *is* thinking, writing *is* analysis, writing *is* indeed a seductive and tangled *method* of discovery" (2005, p. 967, emphasis in original). In other words, the analysis does not stop when the coding process is completed. Indeed, the longer I was out of the field the more I felt stripped of my insider status, and certain meanings changed in relation to the overall narrative. I deliberately left the story open-ended during the writing process for this reason, and did not reach closure until I was writing the fourth chapter. This is perhaps indicative of the ontology of the research that I outlined in the previous chapter; the unpredictable and contextual process with which affect and immateriality operate counters the legacy of mainstream social sciences which have been built on an obsession with standpoints, fixed ideas, claims, and concepts (Massumi 2015). Indeed, one of postmodernism's great lessons is that foundations of 'truth' are contingent, and so are affects. This study, therefore, could be described as postmodern critical research, because, in the words of Joe Kincheloe and Peter McLaren (2005, p. 321), "it requires researchers to construct their perception of the world anew, not just in random ways but in a manner that undermines what appears natural, that opens to question what appears obvious".

Indeed, cafés and bars have been written about before, and may even appear "obvious", as Kincheloe and McLaren (2005, p. 321) have noted. In fact, one might even wonder about the paradox of studying luxury brands and capitalist markets in attempting to challenge and confront injustice. By ethnographically examining the 'hip' café and bar culture in Melbourne, alongside critical theories of affect, this book exposes the force of affect in governing behaviour in an economy of desire that has yet to be applied and integrated, outside the restricted arena of affect theory. With this in mind, I hope, first and foremost, in my research to have de-familiarized the familiar mind sphere of cafés and bars in Melbourne, and exposed their well-camouflaged ethics of governing through the mechanisms of affect (Bauman & May 2001).

Data analysis narrative

1 *Affective Labour* is hegemonic, ethical.
2 Affect is contagion-based, e.g. requires multiplied opposing bodies. The industry is abundant because affect has proven to be highly generative through malleable mindsets and imaginations.
3 Affect fetishises hospitality, which as an industry is predicated on contagion (the commodity—money—commodity transaction, etc.) . . . So ever refined (referring to the endlessness of desire).
4 Because of this multiplication of affective variables (enabled through endless refinement), styles and intensities of service become *the* choice—because it's a potentially hegemonic variable/choice, i.e. 'the' thing you choose.
5 Because of this affective objectivity, service and care become less forced and more about meeting the scale of needs than emotional overhaul/transformation.
6 As such, the workers find freedom in the 'realness' and honesty of the job, symbolised in the 'chats' (the spontaneity of interaction). Affect is contagious, so requires opposing bodies, expressed by the staff wanting to be affected back.
7 The industry is predicated on wants/desires, so the workers are simultaneously needed (in the fulfilment of wants/needs; affect) and dismissed (because of the precarious nature of the job and industry, e.g. no contracts). As such, temporality and detachment are justifiably required.
8 The social platform gives way to affirmations of reality; being able to observe strangers, play around with people, read people, are all the ingredients in the production of the affect (and also feed back into the infrastructure of the city).

9 The workers are autonomous inasmuch as you have to be autonomous to be able to deal with spontaneous interactions in a highly accelerated/repetitive context, which is why the business model is hegemonic.

10 Workers burn out: exhausted from temporality (meeting wants and needs) on a shift work basis. An overwhelming amount of participants present beautifully colourful depictions of a world they do not want to be in. But the production of affect is a desired mode—if customers' needs are met, then the workers' needs are met; they're satisfied and it's fulfilling.

11 It seems the workers' needs are only *temporarily* met (personal/private) but their desires seem to burn out.

12 We live in a growing economy of desire, but desire doesn't correlate with what's good for us (desire is hegemonic). Ethics vs. desire.

13 Having a temporal mindset (the ability to move freely in the present) is synonymous with autonomy, because the embrace of informal chat, shift work, precariousness generally, reflects or happens because of the job's grounded, honest, largely un-scripted nature.

14 Spontaneous presentation of affect—which is the satisfaction of customers' needs/wants—is autonomous, and drives the hegemonic business model. The temporal mindset (freedom of degrees of movement) is one of the drivers of accelerationism.

15 At what cost can the production of desires (which requires autonomy) emancipate its workers?

16 It appears emancipation exists, but on a temporal level and not a stable state. Emancipation is momentary.

17 The fact that "everyone should do hospitality *for just a day*" has been said by so many staff indicates the deeply fleeting nature of affective empowerment: just one day in the industry has the power to change your mind, affect you so much that you'll be able to 'see things differently', one fleeting affect at a time.

18 The never-ending quest for advancing modes of meeting desires, the fleet-footedness of it all (affect), is hegemonic both internally and externally, and the endless refinement happens alongside the embrace of temporality and autonomous day-to-day behaviour (emancipation).

19 Capitalising on 'the moment'.

Interview questions

1 How long have you worked for this company? What was your job before this one?
2 Age?
3 What is your role in this company?
4 How much do you get paid?
5 Is this your only job?
6 What is Melbourne hospitality to you? Do you think it is unique?
7 Do you feel respected and treated fairly in your job?

8   Are you aware of the presence of others (customers) while you are at work?

9   Do you feel like you are part of team or are you more self-directed in your job?

10   Why have you chosen to work in this particular field?

11   What gets you through the hard days at work?

12   What is your favourite and most hated aspect of this job?

13   Do you feel that you have much freedom and autonomy in this job? If so is that a good thing?

14   Does work leave you once your shift has ended, or does it figure in other areas of your life?

15   Do you socialise with any of your co-workers? Why, or why not?

16   Who/what organisation do you consider to be responsible for your wellbeing in the job market?

17   Are there any techniques that you deploy when dealing with customers at work?

18   Do you define your job, or does your job define you?

19   What are your occupational goals? If you were going to leave your job, what would be the key reason for leaving?

20   Is there anything you would like to add to our conversation?

Reference list

Bauman, Z & May, T 2001, *Thinking Sociologically*, 2nd edn, Blackwell Publishing, Oxford.

Davies, CA 2008, *Reflexive Ethnography: A Guide to Researching Selves and Others*, 2nd edn, Routledge, London & New York.

Ezzy, D 2002, *Qualitative Analysis: Practice and Innovation*, Allen & Unwin, Crows Nest.

Kincheloe, JL & McLaren, P 2005, 'Re-Thinking Critical Theory and Qualitative Research', in *The Sage Handbook of Qualitative Research*, 3rd edn, eds. NK Denzin & YS Lincoln, Sage Publications, Los Angeles, London & New Delhi, pp. 303–342.

Madden, R 2010, *Being Ethnographic: A Guide to the Theory and Practice of Ethnography*, Sage, Los Angeles, London, New Delhi, Singapore & Washington DC.

Massumi, B 2015, *The Politics of Affect*, Polity, Cambridge, Oxford & Boston.

Richardson, L & St. Pierre, EA 2005, 'Writing: A Method of Inquiry', in *The Sage Handbook of Qualitative Research*, 3rd edn, eds. NK Denzin & YS Lincoln, Sage Publications, Los Angeles, London & New Delhi.

Statistics New Zealand 2013. 'A Century of Censuses – Population'. Available from: www.stats.govt.nz/Census/2013-census/profile-and-summary-reports/century-censuses-population/density-most-populated.aspx [2 January 2017].

Index

adaptability 5
adequacy 13–14, 55
affect, and emotion 10–14
affected labour 15, 16, 42, 46, 47, 49, 51, 53, 54, 57, 62, 67, 70, 78, 86
affective labour 8, 9, 10, 31, 37, 50, 71
atmosphere 27–28, 44, 75
authenticity 78
autonomy 69–70
awkward people 58
axial coding 84–85

bar, as a barrier 48–49
Bauman, Z. 82
Beck, U. 2
Bell, D. 25
bifurcation 12
biopolitics 8
Boltanski, L. 2
bondage 55
Bourdieu, P. 37
breaks 41
Broadsheet 80, 81

call centre workers 6–7
Carah, N. 9–10, 31, 52–53
career trajectory 62–65
Carnera, A. 55
cause 55
Chiapello, E. 2
Clough, P. 11
coffee houses 26
commercialisation 20–21
common-sense knowledge 24–29
communicative enclosures 10, 52–53
competition 20, 22–23
contagion, emotional 10, 48
Cowan, T. 77
creative industries 62

cultural content of a commodity 8, 38
customers 15, 25, 34–47; fitting in 42–46; forceful 26; gauging of 34–37, 54, 56–57, 76; 'hip' interactional ecology 37–42; initial encounter 34–37, 53–54
cynicism 3–4

data analysis 83–86; narrative 86–87
deep acting 6
de-familiarising the familiar 82
Deleuze, G. 11–12, 55
desires 12–14
detachment 9, 14, 15, 53–57, 70, 74–75, 83
dispositif 9, 24
disruption culture 29, 70, 71
Durkheim, E. 10

ecologies of interaction *see* 'hip' ecologies of interaction
efforts, labour 38–41
emotional contagion 10, 48
emotional labour 6, 36, 38, 71
emotions 70; affect and 10–14
endless product refinement 22–23
ephemerality 14, 15–16, 65–67, 70, 74–75
equivalence, principle of 3–4
experience 51–52
extraversion 57–58

feeling rules 28, 36
first encounters 34–37, 53–54
fitting-in 42–46
Fitzroy 21
flexibility 5, 30, 31, 69–70
Foucault, M. 8, 11
free love economy 77
freedom 69–70
Freud, S. 11

gauging of customers 34–37, 54, 56–57, 76
gentrification: 'hip' gentrification of
    precarious work 74–79; in Melbourne
    20–21
Giddens, A. 2
gig economy 78
Gill, R. 4, 62
Goffman, E. 6, 10
gratification, demonstrations of 43
Gregg, M. 7–8, 23, 25

Habermas, J. 26
habitus 37, 42–43
Hardt, M. 4, 5, 7, 8, 30, 44, 71
'hip' ecologies of interaction 14, 74–75,
    78; detachment 9, 14, 15, 53–57, 70,
    74–75, 83; ephemerality 14, 15–16,
    65–67, 70, 74–75; transparency 9, 14,
    15, 37–42, 46, 48, 70, 74–75, 76
'hip' hospitality culture 1, 14, 15, 19–33;
    common-sense knowledge in 'hip'
    spaces 24–29; unpredictability and
    production in 'the moment' 29–32
Hochschild, A. 6, 28, 71
hostguesting 25, 46

identification with the workplace 67–71
immaterial labour 7–10, 31–32, 38, 69
immaterial ('in the moment')
    production 75; ascendancy of 7–10;
    unpredictability and 29–32
inadequacy 13, 14, 55
industry networks 45–46
informational labour 7–8, 9
initial affect 34–37
innovation 22–23
interactional ecologies *see* 'hip' ecologies
    of interaction
interactional skills 51–52
interviews 82–83; questions 87–88
investment, personal 16, 67–71

Jameson, F. 58–59

Kinchaloe, J. 86
knowledge, common-sense 24–29

labour efforts 38–41
Lasch, C. 2
Lazzarato, M. 9, 32, 38, 69
life-value 7–10, 32
lifestyle websites 80, 81
living labour 4
living in the present 6–7

Lloyd, A. 6–7, 37, 68–69
love: labours of 77; vocabulary of 62–64
Lyotard, J.-F. 2

'magic' 25, 26
Marx, K. 6, 10, 50
Massumi, B. 5, 12, 27, 67, 70–71, 74, 78
May, T. 82
McLaren, B. 86
Melbourne: 'hip' hospitality culture
    1, 14, 15, 19–33; Melbourne-style
    cafés 19–24; research field 80–81
mental elevation 48–53, 58, 59, 60
militarisation 30
misrepresentations 54, 57–60
modifications 12–14
'moment, the' 5, 70–71, 76, 77–78;
    production in 7–10, 29–32, 75;
    thinking in 35
mood economy 3, 76

narrative biography 2
'nature' 50
negative encounters 52
Negri, A. 4, 5, 7, 8, 44, 71
neoliberalism 2–3, 69, 78
networks, industry 45–46
nonessential industry 22

observation 81–82
O'Connor, J. 24
ontological insecurity 2
open coding 83–84

pain 12–14
pantomime dynamic 40–41
Papadopoulos, D. 4–5
parody 40–42, 58–59
participant observation 81
pastiche 57–60
people-watching 34, 49
personal investment 16, 67–71
Picasso, P. 74
pleasure: pleasure-seeking behaviour 7;
    Spinoza and the desire for 12–14
positive encounters 63–64, 65–66
postmodernity 1–7
post-structuralism 11
Pratt, A. 4, 62
precariat, rise of the 78
precariousness 4–5, 69; 'hip' gentrification
    of precarious work 74–79;
    unpredictability and production in 'the
    moment' 29–32

Taylor & Francis Group
an **informa** business

Taylor & Francis eBooks

www.taylorfrancis.com

A single destination for eBooks from Taylor & Francis
with increased functionality and an improved user
experience to meet the needs of our customers.

90,000+ eBooks of award-winning academic content in
Humanities, Social Science, Science, Technology, Engineering,
and Medical written by a global network of editors and authors.

TAYLOR & FRANCIS EBOOKS OFFERS:

A streamlined
experience for
our library
customers

A single point
of discovery
for all of our
eBook content

Improved
search and
discovery of
content at both
book and
chapter level

REQUEST A FREE TRIAL
support@taylorfrancis.com

 Routledge
Taylor & Francis Group

 CRC Press
Taylor & Francis Group

For Product Safety Concerns and Information please contact our EU
representative GPSR@taylorandfrancis.com
Taylor & Francis Verlag GmbH, Kaufingerstraße 24, 80331 München, Germany

www.ingramcontent.com/pod-product-compliance
Ingram Content Group UK Ltd.
Pitfield, Milton Keynes, MK11 3LW, UK
UKHW020945180425
457613UK00019B/528